"When a man like Don Morgan with his remarkable experience of building a great New England church sits down and shares his secrets, it's time to stop what you're doing and devour his words. This is a man who knows how to take a dying organization and, with God's power, breath life back into it. I watched him do it, and this book tells the story."

Gordon MacDonald, speaker, senior fellow
Trinity Forum, Belmont, New Hampshire
Author of best-sellers *Ordering Your Private World* and
When Men Think Private Thoughts

"This book is a real winner—written from the heart and mind of an admirable, wise, and experienced veteran in the ministry. I highly recommend that every pastor and church leader read it and apply the powerful principles to their own life and ministry."

Dr. Walt Kallestad, senior pastor
Community Church of Joy, Glendale, Arizona

"Don Morgan is one of the most gifted pastors of our time—someone who's been there and done that. If you want your church to grow in numbers, ministry, mission, and outreach, this book is for you."

Dr. Bruce Larson, pastor emeritus
University Presbyterian Church, Seattle, Washington

"Don Morgan has received illumination from the Lord. The years he spent in pastoral ministry provides the twenty-first century church a note of encouragement. In *Share the Dream, Build the Team* there is an apostolic resonance. The call to vision, commitment, passion, compassion, openness to change, and perseverance rings clear. It's a call for more leaders who have received a revelation to make a resolution that will cause a positive revolution in their ministry. This book is a must if revitalization and revival is what you seek."

Dr. LeRoy Bailey, Jr., senior pastor
The First Cathedral, Bloomfield, Connecticut

"I've known Don Morgan for a long time. He is one of the truly committed and successful ministers of our time. As a pastor, he is living proof of what leadership can do to revitalize and renew a congregation. Read this book and discover the 10 key principles to bring new life to your church."

Dr. Robert H. Schuller, senior minister
Crystal Cathedral and Hour of Power Ministries, Garden Grove, California

"If there ever was a team builder my friend Pastor Don Morgan is that person. He's demonstrated the skill of taking his personal dreams and working with a congregation to build a team to see God's work flourish—for the glory of God and His church."

Dr. Fulton W. Buntain, senior pastor,
Life Center, Tacoma, Washington

"Dreams and visions are the language of the Holy Spirit. Don Morgan encourages us to listen, learn and live our dreams. That is good advice from one of the Church's best dreamers. You will love this book."

Dr. Tom Garrott Benjamin, Jr.
Light of the World Christian Church, Indianapolis, Indiana

"*Share the Dream, Build the Team* is filled with helpful advice and practical ideas for ministers who want to revitalize an old church or begin a new one. I heartily recommend it."

Otis Young, senior minister
First-Plymouth Congregational Church UCC, Lincoln, Nebraska

"Don Morgan was 'vision casting' and 'team building' before we knew what to call such actions. Morgan fills this book with unusual wisdom, expressed with unusual clarity."

George Hunter, III, dean
E. Stanley Jones School of World Mission and Evangelism
Asbury Theological Seminary, Wilmore, Kentucky

"Everything written in this book is absolutely true and incredibly helpful for either transforming or maintaining an exciting congregation. I know because after five years since Don handed me the baton as his successor, these keys are still bearing fabulous fruit making First Church a 'WOW' congregation, where the Spirit is alive and miracles happen constantly."

J. Jey Deifell Jr., senior minister
First Church of Christ, Wethersfield, Connecticut

"Where are we going? is a question confronting many mainline churches today. Dr. Donald Morgan, longtime minister of one of America's oldest and most dynamic churches, answers that concern with a model for church revitalization and growth. Through his discovery of a latch missing from the front door of his historic church, shared experiences of how to keep disgruntled members on the team, and an exploration of new ideas in church advertising, Don shows us how to open the front door of the church to our own communities and beyond."

Rev. Dr. Edward "Ted" Robinson, senior minister
Central Union Church, Honolulu, Hawaii

"Don Morgan invested his entire career in the trenches as a very savvy practicioner. This wise sage who stayed the course delineates with clarity those critical ingredients that go into the making of a vibrant apostolic, missional church. Morgan brings a very authentic word about the peaks and valleys of building a Christ-centered church bent on transforming lives. *Share the Dream, Build the Team* contains great pearls from a man who is both self-aware and self-defined."

Blair K. Anderson, senior pastor
Lord of Life Church, Ramsey, Minnesota

Share the Dream, Build the Team

Ten Keys for Revitalizing Your Church

Donald W. Morgan

Baker Books

A Division of Baker Book House Co
Grand Rapids, Michigan 49516

Published by Baker Books
a division of Baker Book House Company
P.O. Box 6287, Grand Rapids, MI 49516-6287

Printed in the United States of America

Library of Congress Cataloging-in-Publication Data

Morgan, Donald W. (Donald Walker), 1925–
    Share the dream, build the team : ten keys for revitalizing your church /
Donald W. Morgan
      p.   cm.
    Includes bibliographical references (p.).
    ISBN 0-8010-9115-2 (cloth)
    1. Church growth—United States. 2. Protestant churches—United
States. I. Title.
BR526.M67 2001
253—dc21   2001025885

For current information about all releases from Baker Book House, visit our web site:
http://www.bakerbooks.com

To my parents—
Eugene Leslie Morgan
my father
who modeled decency and faithfulness
and
Alma Holden Morgan
my mother
who taught me the love of God

also
to my brothers—
Wayne Thayer Morgan
and
Harold Doubleday Morgan
who have always been on my team

Contents

Foreword

This book addresses two of the most important church-planning questions in American Protestantism today. First, what must we recognize as the number one component of a denominational strategy to fulfill the Great Commission?

From my perspective, the answer is clear. We must focus on the renewal of those congregations founded before 1960 that consist of an aging and numerically shrinking constituency but have the potential for a bright future. The old congregational culture that provides a hospitable environment for nostalgia, pessimism, internal criticism, and a powerful attachment to the status quo must be replaced. We must create a new congregational environment; one that rewards creativity, encourages innovation, stimulates optimism, welcomes a venturesome spirit, and demotes care of the real estate from a top priority to a means-to-an-end status. The new top priority is reaching, attracting, welcoming, serving, and assimilating newcomers.

This is the strategy Don Morgan presents. Nearly every observer of contemporary American Protestantism agrees that renewal of old congregations is central to the future of every denomination. They also agree, as the author points out, that the key ingredient is skilled, effective, and visionary leadership.

Second, what is the most challenging assignment for a parish pastor in the scene of contemporary religious culture?

High on that list is planting a new congregation that will be self-expressing, self-governing, self-financing, self-propagating, and averaging at least three hundred at worship by its third birthday. One-half of all new American Protestant missions do not live to celebrate their seventh birthday. Even more difficult assignments are the productive merger of two long-established small churches and transformation of small rural congregations founded before World War 1 into vital and vigorous exurban churches. Next to the most difficult of assignments is to be the fourth or fifth pastor in the history of a ten-to-fifteen-year-old mission. Usually, when founded, such missions encompassed the potential to become large churches, but many plateau with an average worship attendance of 85 to 150.

The most challenging assignment of all, however, is for a pastor to lead the renewal of the demoralized, aging, and numerically shrinking congregation founded many decades ago. This book is a case study in how that mission can be accomplished. Not only that, but in this case it was accomplished in what is clearly the one religious culture most resistant to church renewal—the northeastern region of the United States. Beyond presenting the fascinating autobiographical account of an isolated success story, Morgan identifies the basic principles that are the foundation for renewal. These include the conviction of a calling from God and a passion to respond to that call. Also foundational are enthusiastic, optimistic, and visionary leadership, persistence, hard work, patience, discontent with the status quo, and the capability to effectively challenge people to tackle what they believe cannot be done.

But if the renewal of aging congregations should be the number one component of a denominational strategy, why does it happen so rarely? The answer is that 95 percent of today's pastors do not bring the gifts, skills, passion, and persistence required for that most difficult assignment. This book is based on the assumption that those principles and skills can be identified, taught, learned, and practiced. This is not simply one more case study in church renewal. It is a manual that identifies core competencies required to fulfill the most difficult pastoral assignment in contemporary American Protestantism.

Pessimists are right! They do not possess the resources required to transform the life of what everyone (insiders and outsiders) agree is a dying church. Only with God's help and the leadership of a visionary pastor—one who knows how to enlist allies—will that transformation be accomplished.

Lyle E. Schaller
Naperville, Illinois
November 2000

Introduction

Why This Book?

I'd been pastor only a few months. The old, historic church I'd come to serve had been declining in membership the previous eight years. Could I turn it around? Could I make a difference? Could I provide the kind of leadership that would confound all the grim predictions I had been hearing? Could this Connecticut church be revived to become a vital testimony of faith?

One day while walking along the sidewalk across the street from the church—its gorgeous colonial Meetinghouse eye-catching to all—I passed a young man, apparently a tourist. He stopped, turned toward me, and gesturing toward the church, asked, "Tell me, sir, is that a church or a museum?" The question was understandable since this was a historic town, but the implications were devastating to me.

Immediately, with controlled but no less fervent passion, I exclaimed, "I hope to God it is a church!"

But the issue is identical for many churches today—are we a church or a museum? A lively mission for Christ or a moribund, struggling testimony to the past?

The Critical Moment

Early in my ministry I had occasion to ride with a businessman who was an older and highly respected member of the First Church of Christ in Wethersfield, Connecticut. We were going to a meeting in the city adjoining our town. On the way, this man questioned me warmly but searchingly. Knowing I was new on the job, he was trying to size me up; at the same time, he probably wanted to express his doubts in order to give me fair warning.

The man began by reminding me that our town had plateaued in population. The postwar boom in this suburb was over. Not only that, but the Protestant population was declining, he reminded me. Given those grim statistics, he asked, "Is it reasonable or realistic to think the church can grow?"

"Absolutely!" I responded, believing I was right. His expression was courteous but unconvinced.

Desiring to be well schooled in the history of the church, I read the minutes of annual meetings held during the period of decline prior to my arrival. At one meeting, I found there had been considerable discussion concerning the loss of members and the reduced numbers of people attending worship. A staff member had explained the same thing was going on in mainline churches, and that continued decline should be expected. I was struck by the ease with which that statement was made and its acceptance by the congregation. It seemed that since this was the way things were going to be, they might as well sit back and watch what happened.

Another event that brought home to me the state of affairs took place at my first property committee meeting. One item on the agenda was to consider what should be done with the Marsh Building, an adjoining parish house named after a former pastor who had served with distinction during the American Revolution. Two proposals were placed on the table: rent the building to some outside group or sell it. Prior to that moment, I'd heard nothing about giving up one of the buildings. But in the discussion, it was acknowledged that the Marsh Building was receiving little use with the decline of activities and numbers of people.

"Why not get rid of it?" someone reasoned.

Not only was I stunned, I was alarmed that my hopes and plans would be stymied by the loss of the facility. I wondered what I should say. Most of the members present—all men—were in the world of business. Somehow I knew I must speak out in a way they would understand. I sensed this was a critical moment.

"Gentlemen," I began as the Lord led me, "before you reduce our production facilities, check our shipping schedule."

The talking stopped. There was a moment of thoughtful silence. I sensed the committee was getting the message.

"You mean," asked one committee member, "that we will need that building?"

"Precisely!" I answered. "In fact," I added, "someday we may need more buildings and more space, not less."

"You mean," inquired another, "we are going to grow?"

"Yes," I responded.

After a pause, one of the committee members proposed that the matter be tabled. It was, unanimously—and forever.

Some years later, two of the committee members independently told me they will never forget that moment or my words. My remarks had registered with them, and as good businessmen they accepted the intent. In fact, they allowed, their respect for me went up several notches that evening. They sensed a new era had begun, not of defeatism, but of hope.

Could the church change? Would it change? Someone has put the question like this: Are we fishers of men or keepers of an aquarium? I intended that we would be fishers of men. I believed that the Lord had called me to the Connecticut church, not to complacently preside over increasing stagnation, but to lead it into an era of renewed vitality and growth.

Expect Great Things

What followed over the years was confirmation of my hopes. The church turned around. It ceased losing and started gaining members at an increasingly rapid rate. The Sunday morning attendance grew. In time, we required three services, not just one.

Today that church is the fourth largest in the denomination nationwide and the largest in the Northeast. Its attendance is five times what it was when our work began. Most significantly, it is recognized as one of the most dynamic and spiritually alive churches in the entire region. It happened because, in the words of one of my heroes, William Carey, we set out to "expect great things from God, attempt great things for God." Great things happened!

That is the reason for this book. Too many churches, and too many pastors and church leaders surrender to despair, accepting their less-than-flourishing situation. They see no hope for improvement or for their church to be a lively, dynamic, effective outpost for the kingdom. I do not and cannot believe that is God's will. I do not and cannot believe that is what Christ wants. In fact, years ago, having taken on several difficult situations and witnessing a major turnaround for each, I came to the realization that this was what the Lord wanted me to be about. He was calling me to be a witness to the possibility of revival in churches, whatever their situation.

In the chapters that follow, I set forth principles I believe are basic to seeing a church come alive. They are the central concepts for being what I would call an apostolic church, the kind of church described in the New Testament, growing in times of pluralism and in a hostile culture, not too different from the times in which we find ourselves.

My own passion is that Christ's church can be as great and transforming a force in the twenty-first century as it was in the first century! If what follows here helps any pastor, church leader, or church member to realize God-given potential and serve the purposes of the King, I shall be glad. This much I know: It can happen!

1

Where There's a Will

So where do you begin as the pastor of an ailing church? You begin with yourself. Who are you? Where do you stand? What do you believe? What are your expectations, your convictions, your dreams? What can you bring to the situation? Whether you like it or not, you are the key to something exciting happening in and through your church.

I heard a lawyer once comment about a certain church struggle. Perhaps he was giving legal counsel in the midst of its situation. "I would think," he said, "that the shepherd should lead the flock, not the flock lead the shepherd."

However you interpret it, that comment is certainly true. The pastor is, or should be, the key player. He or she should provide leadership. The shepherd should lead the flock and not wait for the flock to lead.

The evidence is strong that the pastor plays the determining role in a growing, vital church. All great churches have a visionary pastor providing the leadership. A pastor might wish to downplay the role, but cannot. The pastor is the key.

Some would dispute this. Some pastors belittle their role or fail to see what they, in fact, bring or fail to bring to a church. Some pastors prefer to identify the process as key, or anything else that takes the spotlight off themselves. While the humility is admirable, it misses the point and obscures the truth.

A pastor's expectations, style, and convictions matter enormously. Look at some of the great churches of our time. Highlight Willow Creek, and there looms Bill Hybels. Highlight Saddleback, and there looms Rick Warren. Highlight Community Church of Joy, and there looms Walt Kallestad. Without the key role these pastors played, phenomenal churches never would have happened.

So what do such pastors bring to the table? A style, a passion, a vision, and a faith that impel extraordinary churches. While you or I may not feel we're in the same league, there's no escaping that point. The pastor's leadership is key to the dynamic extraordinary church. As God uses the well-known pastor in a mighty way, God can use you and me too. The work begins with you, and it begins with me.

What, then, is your will for your church? For where there's a will, remember, there's a way. And when your will is in the will of God, then surely there is a way. Growth can happen; it will happen.

Why are these issues so central? Because church leaders and pastors have so many ways to avoid responsibility for the kind of leadership they give or fail to give. Real soul-searching is in order before much can happen. Examine your attitude, assumptions, inclinations, and even your excuses. Only then can you prepare, and allow the Lord to prepare, the kind of leader a vital church requires.

Numbers Count

Some—no, many—say, "Numbers don't count," or "I'm not interested in numbers." Really?

Numbers are not just numbers—they signify people, and presumably we who are in the service of Jesus Christ care about people. Presumably we care about their welfare, well-being, and how the gospel might bless their lives. We care if people are being neglected or turned off by the church.

Jesus spoke of numbers all the time. He fed the five thousand—that's a number, and the disciples thought there was significance in that number. Presumably the five thousand counted. Maybe the disciples said, "Wow, Jesus! Look at that!"

Jesus spoke of the ninety and nine and the one—note the one!—lost sheep. How would a good shepherd know one sheep was missing? Because he would count and keep counting. Counting is important if you're a good shepherd. If you don't count, if numbers are unimportant, you're not much of a shepherd or up to the job!

Notice the attention the early church gave to numbers. Why, the first Christians were counting all the time. They delighted and celebrated the great and increasing numbers coming into the movement. They saw this as evidence of the vitality and growing power of the church and the working of the Holy Spirit. They took it as a sign of God's faithfulness and of their faithfulness. They weren't indifferent to this. They rejoiced in it.

Read Acts 2:41: "That day about three thousand souls were added to them."

Or Acts 2:47: "And the Lord added to the church daily those who were being saved."

And Acts 4:4: "However many of those who heard the word believed; and the number of the men came to be about five thousand."

Plus Acts 5:14: "And believers were increasingly added to the Lord, multitudes of both men and women."

The point of all this? We cannot escape the clear message, that for Jesus and the early church, numbers mattered, and mattered enormously—because numbers are people, and people matter to God.

Another thing we sometimes hear from those indifferent to enlarging the body of believers and having a growing church is this: "I'm not interested in quantity. I'm interested in quality." Sounds good! Supposedly this statement dismisses the issue real quick! It can be even intimidating.

But not so fast. Is it either/or, or is it both? Maybe there's an inherent connection between quantity and quality in churches. Maybe you can't have one without the other.

If you study the most vital, dynamic, and growing churches, you will discover that where there is numerical growth, there usually is spiritual growth. Those who dispute this haven't looked closely and let themselves off too easily, excusing their inertia.

Perhaps surprisingly, the fact here is what I found in our fast-growing church. As more and more people came into the life of our church, they brought new vitality to our life of faith together. Not complacent, not satisfied with things as they used to be, they brought a dynamic that pushed us forward toward greater faithfulness and spiritual growth. The more we added to our flock, the higher the commitment of the church as a whole. We moved, in fact, from being a low-commitment church to being a high-commitment church. I confess, I found it exciting and deeply satisfying, though no less challenging.

In a word, the increased quantity brought increased quality.

Rick Warren, in his superlative book *The Purpose-Driven Church,* reminds us that we are called to be faithful and fruitful—not one or the other, but both. "God," Warren asserts, "wants your church to be both faithful and fruitful. One without the other is only half the equation. Numerical results are no justification for being unfaithful to the message, but neither can we use faithfulness as an excuse for being ineffective."[1]

Why is it so important to say all this? Because you need to rid yourself of any crippling, impeding, self-defeating assumptions, notions, and—yes—excuses. As long as you harbor such views as "numbers don't count" or you're only interested in faithfulness and not fruitfulness, you will lack the passion and the drive to see your church flourish. You'll content yourself with less than your best for the Lord. You'll justify and excuse your complacency. You'll bear little or no fruit in the Lord's vineyard.

Somewhere, sometime, you need to come to grips with the Lord's clear and compelling statement to Peter, and, I believe, to you and me, as recorded in Matthew 16:18: "On this rock I will *build* My church [italics mine]." Surely he is interested in his church growing and reaching more and more people. Surely he envisioned his movement as an ever-expanding reality by which more and more lives might be touched and transformed. How then can any follower be content with a dormant, less than effective situation for the cause of Christ? How can any disciple dismiss ineffectiveness as of no consequence?

Somewhere, sometime, it's important to come to grips with our Lord's final and absolute command to his disciples, as recorded in Matthew 28:19: "Go therefore and make disciples." He didn't say, "Recycle the saints," or "Simply care for those already there," although he surely did call upon us to feed his sheep. No, Jesus said, "Make disciples." Be fishers of men and women, not keepers of the aquarium. Be engaged in a mission, not a chaplaincy.

The mission comes down to you and me as pastors and church leaders. What do we regard as important? What do we believe is the nature of our calling? What is the will of God for his church, and are we in his will?

If you don't believe your congregation is called to be effective, dynamic, and growing for the kingdom, none of these vital signs will happen—count on it! What follows in these pages will be of little use; you can stop now because, without realizing it, your doubts and *laissez-faire* attitude are roadblocks to what the Spirit of God can do. Nothing will happen.

But if you have the will to see your church grow, to help it become dynamic, and if you see yourself called, not only to have the will, but to be in the will of God, then your congregation can become dynamic. It can! In short, where there is a will there is a way, and when you're in the will of God the way will open.

Jesus at the Helm

Perhaps you accept your role in the dynamic church in such a way that it becomes a heavy burden. You feel you cannot measure up. You cannot take on all that responsibility. There's a danger of taking yourself too seriously. Now don't misunderstand me. Take what you bring to the situation seriously, but don't take yourself seriously. That route, for many, leads to burnout, always a danger for anyone with a passion for their calling and the gospel. Remember, you're not alone. There is one who will do whatever needs to be done, through you and through those around you. With him, the burden is light and the yoke is easy. Just remember, the burden is with him!

Many years ago, while serving another church, I found myself fretful about too many things. I found myself trying to do it all and be on top of every situation. I was burning out. Not only that, I was dead wrong.

I shared with my leaders at a leadership retreat: "I am not at the helm of this church. It is not my job to see that everything happens just as I would have it. Jesus is at the helm. He is in charge. This is his church. I need only release myself to his guiding power and presence. I have decided to just do what I need to do and leave the big picture to him!"

I then told my leaders I was resigning from my role as leader of the church. They were stunned. *What was this all about?* they wondered. I quickly explained I was not leaving and that I would still fulfill my responsibilities. I would preach on Sunday mornings and do the other pastoral things. But in a profound sense, I was stepping aside. From that moment on, I told them, Jesus would be in charge. Jesus would be at the helm. He would make any growth happen! I invited them to join me in following his leading.

You have no idea how liberating this conviction became to me. I was a new man, with a new style. I was a better leader. I would be a joyful instrument in the hands of him who is our Lord and Savior. From that day on, I was, I believe, a far more effective minister. That remained my style and my outlook thereafter and to this day.

You need only conform to God's will, be used of him, and keep attentive to his leading to proceed. Then you can move ahead fully confident that he will assure the success of your efforts for the kingdom.

To see your role as crucial is not to add to your burdens. It's only to say that before you can provide the kind of leadership that will enable your church to be all it can be, get rid of attitudes and assumptions that trip you up. Recognize that you are the key ingredient at the human level. You must be a leader who leads, a shepherd who shepherds. You must have the will and passion to see signs of the kingdom grow where you are, and you must put yourself in the will of God. Get that right and the rest will follow.

Let me conclude this chapter with a prayer written by a lifelong hero of mine, Dwight L. Moody. This was a man who certainly believed that where there's a will, there is—by the mercy of God—a way! Moody had that passion for leadership but also passion to be in the will of God. I've lost count of the number of times or the number of days I've undertaken my labors in the vineyard of the Lord by praying this prayer. I commend it to you:

> Use me then, my Savior, for whatever purpose, and in whatever way, You may require. Here is my poor heart, an empty vessel; fill it with Your grace. Here is my sinful and troubled soul; quicken it and refresh it with Your love. Take my heart for Your abode; my mouth to spread abroad the glory of Your name; my love and all my powers, for the advancement of Your believing people; and never suffer the steadfastness and confidence of my faith to abate—that so at all times I may be enabled from the heart to say, "Jesus needs me, and I Him."

2

Think beyond
the Parameters

The disciples were getting nowhere. They had fished all night with no results. Then Jesus told them to go out farther and let down the nets in deeper waters. They were quick to respond. "No use," they said. "We've already tried everything, but we've caught nothing." Still, this was the Master speaking. You don't say no to him. Better humor him, they decided, go along with him, and let him see how futile it is.

Then the miracle occurred. The disciples sailed farther and let down their nets in deeper waters. Suddenly they were swamped with fish. They were catching so many fish the net was ready to burst, all but inadequate for the load.

This account illustrates the importance of our chapter 2 principle for any church leader: You've got to think beyond the parameters. Open your eyes and mind to possibilities you've never considered. Only then can a church come alive, become vital, and achieve what once seemed impossible. This was what we had to do in the Connecticut church at the start. We had to think new thoughts, see new possibilities, be open to angles and strategies that previously hadn't been considered. We had to think beyond the parameters.

I am reminded of something I happened upon during a commercial flight years ago. I was thumbing through one of those in-flight magazines when, toward the back of the publication, I came upon a puzzle. It had two rows of dots that you were to connect, using only so many straight lines. The challenge seemed simple enough, and I jumped at it. I confess, I don't care for most puzzles, but this seemed like something I could do quickly just for kicks. I soon found, however, I could in no way connect the dots using the few lines allowed. Then before giving up completely, I tried a different approach. I extended the lines outside the dots. It worked! The trick was going beyond the assumed parameters.

Your challenge is to learn to think beyond the supposed limits of your congregation. Think beyond assumptions and self-imposed, self-defeating limitations, and be prepared to go a new way, with new approaches or strategies. Only then will the results be as amazing to us as all the fish were to the incredulous disciples.

Launch into the Deep

The first and foremost parameter our church had to get beyond was the old assumption concerning our target area. Remember the kindly businessman questioning me about the notion that we could reverse the loss of members and begin to grow as a church? Remember he told me the town had plateaued in population and that the postwar boom was over for our community and other suburban communities nearby? Not only that, but he said the Protestant population in our town was declining. Certainly, he implied, growth was impossible, and reaching more people was an idle dream. He sounded a bit like the disciples to Jesus: "Master, we have toiled all night and caught nothing" (Luke 5:5).

Remember, that was pretty much the initial refrain I heard everywhere. Such doubt was expressed early on at an annual meeting. It had become almost an official policy, a foregone conclusion that this church not only would not grow, but that we should expect it to decline.

Though such shrinking parameters were widely accepted, I saw things differently. Why should we limit membership to our small town? *Yes, we must reach all we can there,* I thought, *but why not reach beyond—far beyond?* "Launch out into the deep," was Jesus' command, "and let down your nets for a catch" (Luke 5:4). Why not do just that?

What I saw was the possibility of becoming a regional church, or "magnet church." Why not? People today don't limit their travels to their immediate community. The corner drugstore is a thing of the past. People drive considerable distances for all sorts of things. Just so, more and more people today are ready to travel farther for a church that is alive, dynamic, and filled with the Spirit.

I saw in our church the makings of a possibility that had been ignored. In recent years an interstate highway had been built right along the boundary of our town, and an exit from the interstate had been placed near our church. It would be easy for people to drive from any number of nearby communities, take that exit, and pull in right at the church! In fact, the actual driving time would be quicker for some than to drive to any church in their own town.

We set out—not abruptly, but ever so surely—to cast ourselves as a regional church and to be open and welcoming to people from beyond our town's boundaries. This took some doing, of course. For instance, I tried to be increasingly careful about announcing local events from the pulpit in such a way as to make people from beyond our town feel like outsiders. We had to talk regionally as well as think regionally. We began to refer to our larger community rather than just our town.

In the course of time, with this new concept of our target area—thinking beyond the parameters—and with various other moves to enhance the visibility of what we were doing, people began coming from a much larger area. Some even traveled from the state north of us, Massachusetts. Not just a few would drive for three-quarters of an hour to get to our church. Within a few years, fully half of our membership lived outside our immediate town.

That is what I mean by thinking beyond the parameters. The example above is but one way to go at things differently, to break loose from obsolete assumptions, to see our whole situation in a new and broader light, and to seize opportunities others might never imagine.

May I be frank? This is a principle that cries out for expression in countless churches. As I visit churches, I see little evidence of thinking anew or seizing opportunities readily at hand. Some churches have been fishing all night—fishing for years perhaps—and getting no fish! But do they ask why? Do they take a fresh look at themselves? Are they ready to stand back and examine what they're doing, or failing to do, top to bottom?

Do a New Thing

Whom do you want to reach? Where are they? How can you most effectively reach them? To start, you need to break out of your four walls and your habitual ways. Ask yourself the hard questions. Dare to dream the impossible dream.

Surely you've heard what are called the seven last words of the church: "We never did it that way before!"

But in Isaiah, God says, "Behold, I will do a new thing. Now it will spring forth; shall you not know it?" (Isa. 43:19). Too many churches are not looking for a new thing. They complacently do what they've always done. They do not see the promises of God in their situation, nor are they looking. They do not think beyond the parameters.

If you are the leader of a church or in the leadership ranks, it's your God-given responsibility to be alert to new approaches that can be made. What new ways can be seized? What new thing would God have you do? For only thus can his church prosper, flourish, and reach more and more people for the kingdom.

Years ago I attended a conference on church leadership. Intended for ministers, the material presented concepts from the world of business. The church is not a business, of course, but we can learn from business and from business leaders.

This truth was brought home to me when I was a student in seminary. The membership of the church where I was doing field work included the president of the American Management Association (AMA), Lawrence Appley. One evening during a youth meeting Larry was scheduled to speak. We sat at the back awaiting his turn. Appley prodded me with a thought. "You know what my field is, don't you?" he asked. I acknowledged I did. "Has it ever occurred to you that being a good pastor is to some extent like being a good manager?"

I admitted I'd never thought of it that way.

"Well, it's true," he added. "Think about it." Then he said, "Would you like me to send you some of our AMA materials on management so that you can see what I mean?"

Quickly I agreed, and from that fortunate night gained an appreciation for what can be learned from the business community.

At that conference, I and the others were exposed to a technique advanced by a major business consulting firm. I've forgotten the name of the technique or process, but I do remember the main steps.

Let's say, for instance, you're faced with a problem you can't figure out how to address. First, you must analyze and define the problem as fully as possible. Second, consider the standard or customary ways of dealing with such a problem—ways that probably don't work, or that produce limited results. Third, imagine that in a totally different field you encountered a similar problem. Ask how, given that different frame of reference, such a problem might be addressed and solved.

By this parabolic method of analysis, you'll often see solutions that otherwise never would have occurred to you. *"Voila!"* you exclaim. "That might work! That might do it! Now let's design the program along those lines and develop a strategy in similar form." In such a manner, you will come upon fresh approaches and methods. It's a useful technique for thinking new thoughts and discovering new approaches.

Now, bear in mind, this is a simple technique advanced in high management circles. Eminent companies have paid good money to teach this to their leaders. But what is it, really? It's thinking beyond the parameters, getting out of the ruts. What I am saying here is that the church, if it is to be all it can be for the kingdom and to advance the cause of Christ, needs to be just that creative. Who knows, in such a way God may well lead us to break through and overcome the forces against Christ and his followers.

Robert Schuller tells a wonderful story that fits well what I am saying here: A certain man was fishing when down the bank he noticed another fisherman who seemed to be having considerable success. Then he noticed something peculiar; this other fisherman would carefully measure each fish. If it was small, he kept it. If it was large, he threw it back in the water.

Puzzled, the first fisherman spoke to him, saying, "Excuse me, but I have been watching you. Tell me, why do you keep all the small fish but throw back the big ones?"

"Oh, that's easy," came the reply. "If they are less than ten inches, I keep them. If they are more than ten inches, I put them back. You see, I only have a ten-inch frying pan."

My friend, that sums up what happens in too many churches and in the leadership style on too many fronts. The frying pans are too small! Leaders desperately need to think new thoughts, dream new dreams, obtain new ideas, attempt new strategies, and—above all—think beyond the parameters.

"Launch out and let down your nets," says the Lord.

3

Project a Vision Others Can Catch

Habakkuk 2:1–2 contains this stunning, commanding, and highly suggestive passage:

> I will stand my watch
> And set myself on the rampart,
> And watch to see what He will say to me,
> And what I will answer when I am corrected.
>   Then the Lord answered me and said:
> "Write the vision
> And make it plain on tablets,
> That he may run who reads it."

Here is a wonderful clue as to what God wants of church leaders. Habakkuk, you will recall, was waiting for a vision, trying to make sense of what God wanted from him. He was bewildered as to where events would lead. He needed some revelation and resolved to place himself where the vision might be received. He resolved to be receptive to whatever God might say, and was assured the vision would come. Further, he was told to write it down, make it plain, that others might see it, understand it, and run with it.

To me, the passage tells much about the necessity to receive disclosure from God and to share it. The passage sheds considerable light on the necessity of vision for leaders in God's church. It has often been noted that all great leaders are visionaries, and all great churches have visionaries at their helm. But that isn't the end-all. People know what vision is; people understand it—are alive to it.

Peter Drucker, counselor to business and church leaders alike, writes: "Leadership is not a magnetic personality; that can just as well be a glib tongue. It is not making friends and influencing people; that is flattery. Leadership is lifting a person's vision to higher sights, the raising of a person's performance to a higher standard, the building of a personality beyond its normal limitations."

The key there, I submit, is that real leadership is visionary and all such leadership succeeds in communicating the vision to others. Leaders share the dream and build the team! With that in mind, look at the importance of vision in your role as a leader in God's church and how such vision may be obtained. In so doing, you'll understand this third principle for leading a vital, growing church.

When I completed my first year in our Connecticut church, I delivered a message setting forth the vision that I wanted to share with my people. Why did I wait a full year to do so? There were lots of reasons, but the key one was that I believe people need time to get to know the shepherd's voice. They need time to have a sense of who you are and where you're coming from. Only then will they be receptive to new direction. After a full year of getting acquainted and becoming secure in my role as senior minister, I was ready to share with them my vision for our church.

The Early Church Vision

The title of that message was "The Early Church Experience." Some thought I might speak about the new earlier worship service that had just been introduced, but I wanted to take my people back two thousand years to the early church, the apostolic church, when faith was vibrant, the movement was growing, and people were being reached in astonishing numbers.

In setting forth the chief characteristics of the early church, I relied upon the apt description given by Leslie Weatherhead, that great London minister during World War 2. The description was brought to my attention by another visionary author, Bruce Larson. Weatherhead pointed out six essential characteristics of the first-century church. Citing those characteristics, slightly rephrased, I was giving our congregation my vision of the kind of church we would become.

Transformed by the Living Christ

It all begins with Christ! Something happens to us, something changes us that is an experience of the living God. So it is with all vital and authentic Christianity.

I reminded my congregation of a certain line in the much loved hymn "Amazing Grace." That song points to something precious and all-determining: "The hour I first believed." How well I remember that moment! There needs to be such a moment in our lives when everything falls into place, when we understand, when truly God's presence is felt. That moment is when you welcome Christ into your life, acknowledging your need of a Savior and a Lord. That becomes the watershed of life, the whole flow of life shifts, and you are never the same again. That is the kind of church you're part of, the kind of church you're going to be, a church where people have "a transforming experience of the living Christ."

Passionate to Pass on the Experience

Those early Christians could not hold back. They could not keep to themselves what was happening to them. They could not selfishly hoard the Good News. They did what all normal people unfailingly do when something wonderful happens to them: They share it with others.

No passion is a clue to the sad lack of growth and vitality in many churches in our time. The people in some churches are not on fire with their faith and in all probability are not on fire because their faith is not experiential. Nothing has happened to them at the core of their being. They have not had "a transforming experience of the living Christ."

But the kind of church you are going to be part of is a church where people have a passion to pass on the experience.

Unbreakable in Fellowship and Like-Mindedness

"There is no such thing," declared John Wesley, "as a solitary Christian." Not for a moment did the early Christians see themselves as isolated and alone, doing their own thing, having their own way. They banded together and held together for dear life in Christ. They shared in fellowship. They became one body, a "we." In Scripture, the point is tellingly made: "Now all who believed were together" (Acts 2:44).

Part of that, I told my people, is the importance in today's church of small, sharing, learning, and support groups—something we all need to be a part of. A single ember will die without the company of other embers in the fire. We need from one another encouragement, support, and reinforcement in the finest things of life. Such groups are the key to vital, loving, and alive churches, taking a clue from the early church experience of an unbreakable fellowship. That is the kind of church you can encourage.

Unconditional in Loving All Others

The early Christians reached out with warmth, compassion, and caring. Not for a moment were they "God's frozen people," holding themselves apart, keeping themselves aloof. No, they were debonair folk who went about doing good and overflowing with love for others. As the twentieth-century hymn puts it, "They'll know we are Christians by our love." Warm, outgoing, exuberant love must characterize a vital, growing church today. That's the kind of church you can help grow.

Serene Despite Trials of the Day

Early Christians were a peaceful people, or, to put it differently, they were a people at peace. They were at peace with themselves and at peace with God. They were at peace with themselves *because* they were at peace with God. The reconciling love of God had accomplished it for them. "For He Himself is our peace," said Paul to the Ephesians (Eph. 2:14). No need to fight it! No need to live life troubled by fear and unrest. Come what may, Christ is peace. That's the kind of church you can have.

Joyful beyond Happiness

Those early church people radiated joy. The true followers of Jesus were people of transparent joy. George Bernard Shaw, commenting on Bunyan's Valiant-for-truth, said, "This is the true joy of life, the being used for a purpose recognized by yourself as a weighty one . . . the being a force of Nature instead of a feverish clod of ailments and grievances complaining that the world will not devote itself to making you happy." No, those early Christians were a vital, faith-filled church, and in your time you'll be a community of manifest joy.

So it was that our congregation resolved that worship, along with all other aspects of our life together, would be joyful, not stiff. Our worship would not be dull, deadly, formal, or simply an example of going through the motions. It would not reek with ill-suited dignity, which as Dwight L. Moody once observed, was never listed as one of the fruits of the Holy Spirit. Rather, our worship would be alive, creative, and—above all—joyful. That, I concluded in my sermon, is the kind of church we are, and that is the kind of church we are going to be.

Such were the themes I touched upon again and again, and the vision I had for our church became increasingly understood, claimed, and embraced. That vision became the rallying point for all we would set out to do and become. We were indeed becoming a new church!

Needless to say, it was deeply reassuring when George Hunter, more than a dozen years later in his excellent work *How to Reach Secular People,* observed that our "apostolic approach to secular people helped turn around one of New England's most historic Congregational churches."[1] He rightly understood what our church had been doing. He correctly noted what we had become.

How did that vision come about? Well, it's a long story, and many things happened to me through the years contributing to it. Certain Christian writers expressed what the church needs to be in our time, and profoundly affected me. One of them was my dear friend Bruce Larson and his book *Risky Christianity.* Deeper reading in Scripture helped inform me and shape that vision. But most of all, it was the voice of God speaking to me, changing me as I sought to be faithful to his divine summons. So you as the leader or pastor of your church are to be a visionary. That is your role, your calling.

The Minister's Keys

This brings to my mind a challenging assignment I received one day without warning. It was at the Robert Schuller Institute for Successful Church Leadership. During a luncheon board meeting, Dr. Schuller turned to me and asked me to do him a favor. That afternoon, in fact within the hour, he was supposed to lead a workshop on the role of the senior minister. Something had come up, and he would be unable to keep the commitment. Would I pinch hit for him? What could I say but, with considerable reluctance, "Yes."

Now I had a problem! I had not prepared for this last-minute assignment, but within minutes sixty or more pastors would gather for my address. To begin with, I knew they would be deeply disappointed not to be hearing from Schuller. They would have to settle for me; what a letdown! Further, what would I say? In the half hour that I had time to think about it, I came up with the following keys.

- The senior minister is the **keeper** of the vision. The vision begins here. If the pastor doesn't have it, it's doubtful the church will have it.
- The senior minister is the **communicator** of the vision, charged with the challenging task of making the vision known and accessible. Much of the time an effective pastor will be engaged in communicating the vision.
- The senior minister is the **coordinator** of the vision, responsible to oversee its implementation, helping to shape the life of the church accordingly, and bringing the vision into reality.
- The senior minister is the **celebrant** of the vision, called to affirm, rejoice in, and celebrate the realization of the vision, leading the chorus in praising God!

Though hastily arrived at, those four points summarize fairly well what I believe. They are the dominant concepts that underlie and run through these pages. In a nutshell, this is what it takes to share the dream and build the team!

In the total mix through which the vision comes, central must be the counsel from God. Recurringly, ministers must—in the spirit of Habakkuk—stand watch to see what God will say. For, as Habakkuk (2:3b) goes on to say,

> Though it tarries, wait for it;
> Because it will surely come.

I deeply believe we must be forever open to what the Lord is saying to us. In the context of the written Word and the company of the saints, we must be seeking to know his will in order to be in his will.

Be Specific

One sermon setting forth my vision to my church people would not do it, of course! This was only the beginning. The sharing must be ongoing. From time to time, I would present a position paper to our church board, lifting up the vision in one form or another, pointing out how far we had come but also indicating how far we had to go yet. More and more, we felt the current of change and sensed the unique opportunities the Lord was opening. More and more, a new spirit—the Holy Spirit—seemed at work in our midst. But through it all, the vision was at work. Through it all, the vision gave direction.

Included in those position papers were projections of where we should be at certain points in numerical growth. I told the church board how many people we should expect to add to this body of Christ within, say, the next two, three, and five years. I believed it was important to be specific in such matters as a way of holding ourselves accountable. How else could we know whether we were fulfilling our intention of growth? We should resist the temptation to hide our hopes and to protect ourselves behind ambiguity.

I'll admit it. It was a little scary to be that specific. I found myself inclined to hold back. What if we didn't

make it? What if we failed? Wouldn't this jeopardize my
position with these folks? Why, they might start looking
for a new minister! Then I realized how self-serving and
utterly faithless it was to entertain such timidity. I must
have sufficient faith in what I believed God was doing in
our midst to hold myself and our leaders fully accountable. I would go on record as to our goals. If we failed, we
would know we failed. If we succeeded, we would rejoice
in our success.

Too many churches live in denial on this score. They
will not deal with the facts or look at the clear evidence
that they're failing to fulfill the Great Commission.

Yet a vision is worthy to be embraced for the churches
you lead:

- Not just any vision should be adopted, but an exciting one that captures people's attention. It must evoke
  a "Wow!" because too much with which congregations are confronted and called to undertake is, frankly,
  dull and boring.
- Surely, too, the vision should be challenging. It must
  call forth the best in people and clarify the fact that
  it will take everyone doing their part to succeed. Nothing less will command the response required.
- The vision should be energizing too. It should be sufficient to release the adrenaline in a body of believers
  who are turned on.
- But most of all, a worthy vision should and must be
  God-given! Through persistent prayer, a growing and
  deep biblical awareness, and a spirit of obedience to
  divine will, we should come to the conviction that
  this is what God is calling us to do and to be.

At a certain point several years along in my ministry, the church board adopted this mission or vision statement:

> We are called by the Lord Christ to be a model for our time of the finest and most creative in church life, worship, nurture and outreach; proclaiming a positive, affirming, need-filling faith message; energizing and transforming human lives by the power of the Holy Spirit; and steadily enlarging the body of believers.

Take your cue from Habakkuk. Get into your watchtower and see what God will say to you. What vision will he give? If you wait for it, surely it will come, so you're assured. When it does, it is your task as a leader to write it down. You're to make the vision plain for all to read so they may join the race toward the high calling of God in Christ Jesus. Only then will the thrill be felt and the joy of ministry be experienced!

Of all who have written about the importance of vision in leadership, none has put it better than George Barna, in his excellent book *The Power of Vision:*

> Realize that true ministry begins with vision. For a Christian leader—that is, an individual chosen by God to move his people forward—vision is not to be regarded as an option. It is the insight that instructs the leader and directs his or her path. If, for whatever reason, you are attempting to lead God's people without God's vision for your ministry, you are playing a dangerous game. It is a game that neither pleases God nor satisfies people. . . . Regardless of the cost, get his vision for your ministry.[2]

So each one needs to go about being a visionary leader— if that is one's calling—in terms of personal gifts and in terms of the situation in which one is working. Most needed of all are visionary leaders as the Lord leads and directs. The point is clear: Project a vision and make it one others can catch!

For many years, my favorite and ever-present chair-side book has been *The Imitation of Christ* by Thomas à Kempis. But I would like to share with you the one page that has affected me most profoundly:

> "I will hearken what the Lord God will speak in me."
>
> Blessed is the soul which heareth the Lord speaking within her, and receiveth from His mouth the word of consolation.
>
> Blessed are the ears that gladly receive the pulses of the Divine whisper, and give no heed to the many whisperings of the world.
>
> Blessed indeed are those ears which listen not after the voice which is sounding without but for the Truth teaching inwardly.
>
> Blessed are the eyes which are shut to outward things, but intent on things eternal.
>
> Blessed are they that enter far into inward things, and endeavour to prepare themselves more and more, by daily exercises, for the receiving of Heavenly secrets.
>
> Blessed are they who are glad to have time to spare for God, and shake off all worldly impediments.
>
> Consider these things, O my soul, and shut up the door of thy sensual desires, that thou mayest hear what the Lord thy God shall speak in thee.

4

Go Back to Go Forward

Why step back if you want to move forward? "What sort of double-talk is that?" you may be asking. Sounds paradoxical—and it is! But it's vitally important if you want to lead a church successfully into a new day and a bright future.

This is doubly true if you're leading a church that's been around for some time as opposed to a young or entirely new church—a situation for many pastors and church leaders. Most are not starting from scratch but picking up where others left off. So then, an essential principle of successful leadership in the realization of your vision is just that: Go back to go forward!

You see, before you ever arrived on the scene, your church had a life. Most of the people in your congregation were there long before you appeared. They have memories and loyalties. They have strong emotional ties to the past and aren't likely to receive well a brash young or new leader who comes on the scene and starts talking about a new vision and a new church. In fact, those folk may find it highly offensive, and it's right that they should, because back then, before you came, there were good and faithful people, carrying on within the church they loved and probably feeling very good about it. In a word, you must appreciate the past. In fact, you must build upon and value the past.

If you want to know why many would-be church leaders fail, here's the key: They are so caught up in their own ideas and vision, they don't value what was there before them. They come with lofty dreams, but they make no allowance for the importance of a sense of continuity. They throw out the baby with the bath water, as the saying goes.

The situation's like a well-known and widely read magazine, one of the leading periodicals of its day, that began to lose readership. Something had to be done, so it was revamped to target a different crowd. Suddenly, the editors were trying to reach different readers, and before they knew it, circulation tumbled and they were out of business. Why? Because they focused on readers they did not yet have while neglecting the ones they did have. There was no continuity, no link to the past, and today that magazine is no more! It remains a classic illustration of how *not* to go about change.

Sadly, not a few high-powered, deeply committed, strongly resolute pastors and church leaders proceed like that in a new situation. They do not root their moves in the past. They do not adequately value what's gone before. They pitch their efforts to people they do not have while turning off scores of people they do. To put it another way, they've not taken the time to build a historical foundation. They need to observe this essential principle for leading a vital, growing church: Go back to go forward!

Balance Continuity and Discontinuity

My first semester as a student in seminary I was taught a valuable truth. It was in a class on the ministry led by the president of the seminary—a wise and perceptive man, a leader among leaders. He had national and international stature and important things to share. Thank God I took that class, and happily took note and never forgot one important point made.

The president spoke of the necessary balance between continuity and discontinuity. Both, he said, must be kept in mind, and both, he insisted, were part of the picture in successful leadership. He pointed out that continuity refers to things that don't change, things that give a sense of security and confidence, familiar things, nonthreatening things that link us to the past. Discontinuity refers to things that do change. In fact, it refers to change itself. It's dynamic, fresh, and potentially refreshing. It is necessary for life. People and churches need that.

People need both. Stability and assurance of the familiar give them the sense they're in the right place and all is well. Vitality and creativity, the new and the unfamiliar challenge and stimulate, and people respond to both if offered balance. No one can stay alive if things never change, but no one can handle change unless there's some sense of valuing the past.

Good leadership keeps both in mind—the need for continuity and equally the need for discontinuity. The need for the old, the need for the new. There's assurance in the old, and there's vitality and excitement in the new. But if it's all the one or all the other, the balance is lost and—like that magazine that tried to change overnight—it all blows up in your face.

Notice in Scripture how the new is linked to the old. In his letter to the Romans, for example, Paul carefully roots the gospel—the new—in the past, the history of Israel—the Old Testament. Not only did one Testament inform the other, but they enabled listeners and readers to hold it all together. You could say this is a necessary balancing act that does justice to the truth while understanding the needs of human nature. Everyone needs a sense of the past to make a way securely into our future.

This is something I do not recall being addressed in many books on church leadership. Lots of wonderful ideas and suggestions are made often without adequate counsel and wisdom concerning a great need in all people and established churches. Lacking this, well-intentioned and promising leaders attempt things, then seem to get nowhere, and with disappointing results. The human element hasn't been adequately addressed.

Remember churches are made up of people, and you're dealing with human beings who hurt and have needs and memories. You always need to love and understand them. Someone has said, "It isn't the church, but people who give the church a bad name." Since people make up the church, then, it's people, not things, you need to lead.

Study the Past

To do this, become a student of the past in your church. Acquire a genuine appreciation of the victories that have gone before you. Do as Paul did with such love and sensitivity in his second letter to Timothy: "I thank God . . . when I call to remembrance the genuine faith that is in you, which dwelt first in your grandmother Lois and your mother Eunice, and I am persuaded is in you also" (2 Tim. 1:3–5). Reach back to some of the glory days in your church. And most assuredly, appreciate and celebrate what others—including, I would add, the pastors before you accomplished and did for the kingdom.

I'll admit, sometimes this is difficult to do. You can be so focused on the present and future, thrilled by what you see as the possibilities before you, confident of what you're undertaking in your own time, and inwardly become impatient with people who don't get on board with you as quickly as you'd like. You can seem indifferent to the past or, worse, critical of it.

But if so, you make a big mistake. Worse, indifference smacks of arrogance. It's hardly a quality to be expected in those who follow the loving, compassionate Nazarene who counseled, "Learn from Me, for I am gentle and lowly in heart" (Matt. 11:29).

The solution? Affirm the past as you prepare for the future, and never stop generously affirming what others have done before you, including your immediate predecessor!

This brings me to what I believe was an important element in the revival and renewal of that great church I was honored to lead. How did we apply this recognition of the need for continuity and discontinuity thoughtfully balanced? I mention this because I think you'll find it instructive, and what I describe can be done, one way or another, in any church where you serve.

You need to know a few things to get a picture of the unique situation I faced. For one thing, our church has a long history. When I say "long," I mean long! It was founded or—as they say in historic Congregationalism—"gathered" in 1635. That's just fifteen years after the Pilgrims arrived at Plymouth! It's one of the oldest congregations in the nation and one of the first of three in the state. There's a lot of history there, and it would be clumsy of me to be unmindful of that.

Second, our church is located in New England or, more specifically, in Connecticut, "the land of steady habits," as it's been identified. New England presents a special challenge to vital faith. People there, it's believed, don't express their faith as openly and fervently as in other parts of the country. Some even regard New England as a kind of spiritual wasteland. All of that had to be taken into account— not capitulated to—but taken into account.

Third, my immediate predecessor had served as pastor there for thirty-five years. He'd done marvelous things, was greatly loved, and had overseen several building programs that wonderfully equipped the life of a strong church. In addition, he remained in the community and continued to attend our church. Happily, he's a big-hearted man, not given to interfering and not needing to keep control. He welcomed me warmly, encouraged me consistently, and willingly released the reins of leadership. I valued all that he'd done and often spoke of him as "the one who made it all possible" because of how he'd equipped us in our facilities. His pastorate ended the day mine began. That Sunday, he opened the service and carried it through to a midpoint when he turned it over to me to bring it to its conclusion. He passed the torch to me in the presence of everyone, all in one day!

Naturally, it's difficult for people to shift their loyalties from one pastor to another, especially when the previous pastor has been a familiar fixture for thirty-five years! I didn't resent in the least that he was staying on in town. Nor did I resent his being active in the church. "Who has a better right," I would say, "after a fine ministry of thirty-five faithful years?" It was important to openly express myself in that way, for the sake of maintaining the balance between continuity and discontinuity.

Appreciating the human need to relate to me, the newcomer, my wife and I held an eight-month series of "evenings in the parsonage." Three evenings a week we would have about thirty people into our home for sharing, refreshments, and getting acquainted. Over those months we had a total of about 1,400 people in our home—people who needed this close connection with us to help them move from the past to the future.

I set out to get steeped in the history of our ancient church. Built in 1761, the Meetinghouse had been restored at a cost of one million dollars. I wanted to lift up the richness that could help us move forward. A happy discovery was to learn that Jonathan Edwards, the New England leader of the Great Awakening, had been closely connected to our congregation. When, from 1716 to 1719, he was a Yale student, he lived in our town of Wethersfield, and may have preached from our pulpit on occasion.

In order to reinforce this historic and, for me, exciting link, we commissioned Harry S. Stout, professor of American Christianity at Yale University, to come to our church for a major public lecture. He spoke of Edwards's affirmation of the goodness of God and reaffirmed Edwards's connection with our church. It was a marvelous event, well attended, that lifted up a rich part of our heritage while reintroducing Edwards to our community. It helped to confirm who we were and who we were becoming.

Moreover, Edwards's grandson, Timothy Dwight, had been in our town and worshiped with our people when, as a Yale tutor during the American Revolution, the student body had been evacuated from New Haven to inland towns. Dwight, of course, later became president of Yale and was the key New England figure in the Second Great Awakening. Here was another direct connection to revival and renewal. This was our history! This was our heritage! As we launched into the future and sought to follow the Lord's leading in the reshaping of this great and historic church, we had a rich heritage to draw upon and to celebrate. We were becoming what we'd always been in the deepest sense and in our greatest days. Affirming the past need not hold us back, but rather spur us to become all we could be. We were, in effect, living out our past in new, creative, and exciting ways.

As our past was valued—and for some, resurrected—the congregation began to see the big picture. The people were less likely to resent what we were becoming and far more likely to embrace it with joy, faith, and enthusiasm. We were not a museum, as one young man had wondered, but a vital church, a dynamic mission for Christ while fulfilling our implicit destiny.

Even so, we were living out our vision, taking hold of our dream, becoming an apostolic church in our time. All of that was totally consistent with the heritage of Jonathan Edwards and Timothy Dwight. We were true to it all—the best in the New England faith heritage—and it was exciting.

As we sang the hymn Dwight wrote, we believed in our heart of hearts that he was possibly thinking of our church, our own lovely Meetinghouse, when he set down these beautiful, faith-filled words:

> I love thy kingdom, Lord,
> The house of thine abode,
> The Church our blest Redeemer saved
> With his own precious blood.

I love thy Church, O God;
Her walls before thee stand,
Dear as the apple of thine eye,
And graven on thy hand.

For her my tears shall fall,
For her my prayers ascend.
To her my cares and toils be given
Till toils and cares shall end.

Beyond my highest joy
I prize her heavenly ways,
Her sweet communion, solemn vows,
Her hymns of love and praise.

Sure as thy truth shall last,
To Zion shall be given
The brightest glories earth can yield,
And brighter bliss of heaven.

5

See from the Outside In

Is your church easily approachable? Is it really? Are you sure? If you are going to be a vital, growing church, reaching more and more people for Christ, you had better ask this question, and you had better know the answer.

Many churches and many church leaders give little or no thought to how they come across to outsiders. They assume the best, no doubt. They can't believe they aren't as delightful and charming and irresistible as they fancy themselves to be. Why, people should be coming in droves! They assume that what they have going for them is apparent to everyone. They assume there's nothing about them that might make them the least bit unapproachable. And they assume this at a terrible cost!

Another way to put this is that many churches and many church leaders tend to be myopic. They cannot see outside themselves. They are, in fact, turned upon themselves. Remember the words of poet Robert Burns? "Oh wad some power the giftie gie us, to see oursels as others see us!" Ah, yes, but churches and church leaders cannot do that without standing back and taking a long look—critically and searchingly. If they did, they might make some astonishing discoveries. They might see that, quite unconsciously, they have been defeating themselves and scuttling all their good intentions and efforts.

Let me tell you about a grim discovery I made about my church just five months into my ministry. A frequent practice of mine, something I began doing years before, was to walk up the street toward my church as if I were approaching it for the first time. I shake out of my head any sense of familiarity with the setting. I psyche myself into the perspective of a visitor who has never attended this church. What will I see? What will I notice? What impressions will I have? What feelings will arise within me as I approach this house of God?

As a total stranger, I would not be likely to approach the church as members and frequent attenders do. They know the shortcuts, the interior layout, and will enter doors a newcomer probably would not. One day I went up to the door that would seem to be the logical front door of our Connecticut church. I reached for the handle to open it and let myself in. Then I made a wrenching discovery.

There was no handle on the door! Incredible! I couldn't believe it. *Why,* I thought to myself, *this church is like a speakeasy in the days of Prohibition! You can't get in unless someone on the inside lets you in! What kind of exclusive club is this?*

Almost beside myself with something approaching rage, I ran around the building to go in the side entrance (which, thank God, had a handle) and headed for the office of the associate minister who had served there many years. Surely,

I thought, he would know why there was no handle on the front door of our church.

Five years before, he told me, when our ancient Meetinghouse was restored to its original, pristine form, it had been believed that there had been no handle on the front door when the building was erected in 1761. So in the interest of faithful restoration, no handle was added!

Later, the associate minister went on to say, it was discovered to be a mistake. There had been a handle originally, and it could be installed now without compromising the restoration. This was supposed to have been done, but apparently nobody ever followed through. Apparently it was forgotten, and apparently nobody even noticed. Nobody, at least, until that day—five long years later—when the new senior minister assuming the role of a naïve newcomer, walked up to that door and—no handle!

In those early months of my ministry there, I'd undertaken an advertising campaign for the first time in recent memory at least. With the hope of attracting new people, we were trying to enhance our visibility. As I contemplated the significance of the absence of a door handle, a thought flashed through my mind: How many people, responding to that costly advertising, came to our church only to find they couldn't get in? How many left in frustration? And why? Simply because there was no handle on the front door!

As I was completing the conversation with the associate minister, I asked him if he knew where the absolutely authentic handle for our Meetinghouse could be obtained. He acknowledged that he did since he'd been involved in the restoration project at the time.

I then said, "If you do nothing else in the next few days, will you see to it that such a handle is installed at the earliest possible moment?" He accepted the assignment, and within a week we had a handle on the front door. At long last, people could get into our church!

Now, that episode makes clear how absolutely critical it is to get out of the myopic mind-set and see yourself as others do from the outside in, not from the inside out!

Incidentally, you'll recall that when I began, that church had declined in membership and attendance at a rapid rate. It was this decline, during and after the restoration, we were attempting to reverse. Admittedly, one such omission alone would not account for the losses, but I wonder how much of the decline was due to the simple fact of the lack of a handle on the front door, which through all those years nobody noticed.

What about your church? I'm sure you must have a handle on your front door, but are there other barriers you've never noticed? Are there deterrents you've never detected? Are there subtle negative signals to which you may be oblivious, but which a newcomer quickly senses? Stand back. Take a careful look. Make sure you deal with any potential hindrance to being all you can be for the cause of Jesus Christ!

Work Smarter

I'm convinced the Lord wants you to work smart. He wants you to put on your thinking cap. Remember what he said to the disciples as he sent them out "to the lost sheep of the house of Israel," and how he concluded his instructions? His words are among the most important ever said to the disciples and to all who minister in his name: "Therefore be wise as serpents and harmless as doves" (Matt. 10:16).

If only all who labor in the vineyard of our Lord would remember to show some savvy about the work for Christ!

"Get smart," Jesus would be saying here. "Use your head as well as your heart!"

I find it interesting that the great Jonathan Edwards, in his notable work *The Distinguishing Marks of the Work of the Spirit of God,* emphasizes this same passage to those engaged in the historic revival of his day, the Great Awakening. He reminds his readers, "Be as wise as serpents and harmless as doves," stressing the necessity of being aware and discerning.

May I suggest you use the apostle Paul as a model? He was a superb strategist, marvelously effective in reaching people. In fact, where would the church be without him? He left no stone unturned to fulfill the mission the Lord had committed to him. He knew and practiced this principle of seeing from the outside in, for no barriers were allowed to stand in the way of people coming to Christ.

Remember how Paul put it? "For though I am free from all men, I have made myself a servant to all, that I might win the more; and to the Jews I became a Jew, that I might win Jews; to those who are under the law, as under the law, that I might win those who are under the law; and to those who are without the law, as without the law . . . that I might win those who are without the law; to the weak I became as weak, that I might win the weak. *I have become all things to all men that I might by all means save some*" (1 Cor. 9:19–22 [italics mine]).

This attentiveness of Paul needs to be translated and applied to our times and to our efforts for the gospel. Many churches and many church leaders are astonishingly inattentive to the little, mundane things that get in the way of their mission.

One of the most disturbing situations I ever encountered was when I was called to the home of an older woman, a parishioner, whose married daughter was visiting after going through a horrendous ordeal. With her little girl watching, this young wife had been shot by her husband, who then turned the gun on himself and committed suicide. The shot in her direction had simply grazed her forehead, but her husband had died. When the sudden widow called her church to seek counsel and make funeral arrangements, the person who answered heard what had happened, then incredibly said something like, "Our minister is on vacation and won't be back until the end of the month." That's all she said—nothing more!

The story stunned me. I immediately drove back to my church and gathered all my staff in the office. I told them what had been reported, and deplored the situation. I said, "If a call like that should ever come and I am away while no other minister is available, you must simply respond, 'I will call you back in just a few minutes.' Then call me and I'll tell you what we'll do. But never, never, never leave anyone high and dry like that!"

While you might think no church could be so ill-equipped in its ministry to people, it needs to be said that many churches and church leaders are surprisingly inattentive to the little things that get in the way of fulfilling the mission entrusted to them. They don't see from the outside in; they see from the inside out!

Pay Attention to Detail

However, what if churches and leaders were as on the ball as many secular institutions of our society? We could learn a thing or two, taking a page or more from their policy statements and procedures. For example, Foxwoods Resort Casino is located in southeastern Connecticut on a Native American reservation. It's reportedly the largest casino in the world. I've never been there, but a friend of mine has, and he reported to me how tremendously attentive they were to him from start to finish.

The moment my friend walked in the front door, greeters welcomed him, falling all over him, helping him in any way they could. They graciously led him into the slot-machine room, helped him get seated, and provided him with refreshments. He was told that he should let them know if there was anything he might want. When he left the casino, he received warm good-byes. They told him how delightful it was to have him come and that they looked forward to his next visit. They fairly followed him out to the bus.

My friend isn't a gambler; he assured me of that, and I believed him. He just wanted to see how this place getting such attention in our state (and beyond) was run. Was he ever impressed! He had never been in a place where the entire organization was geared to making it easy for him to come in, play, and to come back. No hindrance was permitted!

Now, friend, if a gambling institution that has no higher purpose than to take your money can pay this kind of attention to details, why can't the church put itself out on behalf of the people it's trying to reach, welcome, and serve? Surely, we must pay closer attention to what we're doing or failing to do. Surely we must see from the outside in.

What subtle barriers stand in the way of your church mission? You may have a handle on the front door, but what may conceivably be tripping you up in ministry? Many churches have inadequate parking facilities, for example. If people can't park easily and conveniently, they can't and won't come in! Adequate parking is as essential as pews or seating. Robert Schuller goes further, saying you need surplus parking: "To any pastor, I make this firm declaration: if your church doesn't have surplus parking, you're hurting. You're paying a high price for this lack of parking! It would be much cheaper for you to buy additional property, to build a high-rise structure or to sell out and relocate on larger property. It would be less expensive for you to do this, with a 20- or 30-year loan, than it would be to struggle along in a dying way as you are today!"[1]

Is there an abundance of clearly marked VISITOR parking at the closest locations of your church? One church I visited had a large parking area but no visitor parking. Let me tell you what it did have: the most conveniently designated parking for the senior minister, the associate minister, the director of Christian education, the church secretary, the church bookkeeper, and the custodian. What does that say? It says to everyone else, "You're less important. We're not concerned about you. Our staff is most important. Their convenience is all we care about."

In my Connecticut church, we permitted no reserved staff parking. We saw ourselves as servants. We parked in the less convenient locations, and managed quite nicely—and were glad to do so. But we did have plenty of visitor parking, as well as parking for the disabled and elderly.

I seem to remember someone saying, "Whoever desires to be first among you, let him be your slave—just as the Son of Man did not come to be served, but to serve, and to give His life as a ransom for many" (Matt. 20:27–28).

Our thoughtfulness in the parking arrangements says what our priorities are.

What unintentional but self-defeating signals do visitors and newcomers quickly pick up when they come on your premises? Keep asking, ever alert to such issues. Is it clear to your newcomers which church entrance to use? Are there clear and highly readable signs communicating, THIS WAY TO THE SANCTUARY or THIS WAY TO WORSHIP? When people get inside your building, is it clear in what direction they should move for whatever they are seeking— church school, nursery, child care, main office, auditorium? The point is, people don't like to look confused or uncertain. It makes them uncomfortable. They aren't interested in playing games. Your job is to make sure they're not put through such difficulty, and to make coming to your church as pleasurable and convenient as possible.

It goes without saying, doesn't it, that church facilities should be fully accessible to the handicapped, as all public places are required to be. It's unthinkable that the church would do less. Ten years ago, I fell down some stairs, ripped my knee apart, and after surgery, had to make my way around with crutches. It's a whole new world, I found. I began to understand what others go through. That's when I saw the sheer necessity of elevators and wide entrances for wheelchairs. My excuses and rationalizations for doing nothing soon faded.

What if someone telephones your church? Is the call quickly answered by a friendly, caring voice? Or does a machine run through a gauntlet of numbers and designations so that you sit there waiting and wondering, *How do I get through?* Maybe there's no answer at all. Has provision been made to assure people of being able to connect with someone in your church?

What if someone in a state of desperation, perhaps even suicidal, calls? Will he or she in that life-or-death moment get a frustrating response? How can anyone excuse such things? What kind of job is being done when it's difficult or impossible to be reached?

Here's something I came upon the other day: "Churches stand ready to help in times of crisis. Or so one may think. The Barna Research Group telephoned 3,764 Protestant churches nationwide and in 40 percent of the calls were not able to get through to anyone, even after calling back as many as twelve times. Half of the churches in the 40 percent did not even have an answering machine. Schedule your crises for eleven o'clock Sunday morning."[2]

What if someone comes into your church office area? Does that person receive a quick, friendly, warm response? Do visitors feel welcomed? Do they get the kind of quick attention they would get at Foxwoods or the Ritz Carlton, or do staff people continue doing their thing, all but oblivious to the person who has entered the room? When staff look up, do they give the impression they wish the intruder would disappear? Sad to say, that's the way it is in some churches.

Are ministers readily available, or do people have to jump through hoops to see one? Who is the church for, after all? Who are the most important people? Those churches and church leaders who function in the bureaucratic mode, as many do, convey the impression that the whole operation is for them, not for those they're called to serve.

I remember calling on a parishioner in a hospital some years ago. She was in a ward, and there were many sick people in the room. Just then a loud and brassy nurse walked in, calling out commands. Obviously she was a supervisor of sorts and wanted everyone to know of her importance, but she had created an enormous disturbance.

I became annoyed with the nurse and her obvious insensitivity to the patients and suddenly spoke up. "Why do you have to make so much noise?" I asked her straight out. "Don't you know these people are sick? These are your patients! They need peace and quiet, not a racket!"

The nurse was visibly taken aback by the fact that someone had the audacity to speak bluntly to her. She quickly grew quiet, then left the room. I sensed the others in that ward were relieved and grateful. Why didn't that nurse conduct herself with greater consideration? In my opinion, she had fallen into the bureaucratic trap that the institution and the staff are there not to serve, but to be served! It happens everywhere.

Make sure your entire staff understands that they are there to serve. We are there in the holy name of Jesus to care about and minister to people.

Little do we realize what obstacles people may experience, even within themselves, as they come to church. A woman once shared with me what she went through. She sat in her car in our parking lot trembling with fear and weeping because something in her background was tormenting her. She almost drove off, she told me. Then she made herself come in, and—in time—found new life.

People carry their own baggage, but you can see to it that nothing—literally nothing—of your doing or due to your failure stands in their way or adds to their burden. You cannot change what fears, insecurities, or hurts people bring, but you can make certain that you're not doing the devil's work through neglect. Thoughtfully, conscientiously, and imaginatively you must make yourself and your church superaccessible and approachable for all.

To that end, share the high resolve of Paul: "I have become all things to all men, that I might by all means save some" (1 Cor. 9:22). To that end, we determine everlastingly to see from the outside in!

6

Lead with an Enabling Style

Just the other day a pastor asked me, "How do you communicate the vision to your people? How do you get it across to them?"

Give that pastor an "A" for astuteness. He was asking a big question. Nothing is more central, more basic, than communicating your vision to others. The reason for this is simple. No one can build a great church alone. You need help; I need help. We need lots of help. We need others who share the dream and help make it happen.

Helen Keller once said, "Alone we can do so little; together we can do so much." Exactly! That's why this principle is utterly central in all we set out to do.

Here is where one's leadership style becomes critical and, in fact, decisive, for the leadership style a pastor brings to his ministry will determine the size of his church. Certain leadership styles mean that a church will always be small.

A church cannot grow if the pastor's leadership style prevents it. Certain leadership styles get in the way. In fact, even if you begin with a larger church, that church will get smaller, conforming to the limited style of leadership a small-church leader brings to it. This will not happen intentionally, of course, but inevitably.

The contrast is sometimes made between the leader or pastor who functions as a shepherd and the one who functions as a rancher. A shepherd can only manage a certain size herd. Beyond that, the situation gets out of hand, becoming unmanageable. A rancher, on the other hand, can and does manage an ever-enlarging herd. He goes at the task before him differently, equipped for growth. In fact, he facilitates and encourages growth.

If your disposition is to micromanage, you automatically impose limits upon what can happen. If you must be in charge of literally everything taking place, and at the center of every decision and every aspect of your church's life, the potential of your ministry will be reduced by self-imposed limitations.

Let's face it, some leaders are insecure. They attempt to control everything, one way or another, openly or subtly. They are paranoid, perhaps, or too easily threatened. They cannot trust people, and worse, cannot trust the Lord. What a pity! For in so doing, they must content themselves with a nongrowing, stagnant, caretaker ministry.

Get out of the Way

Your leadership style counts! Years ago it occurred to me that I could have a church that's like a simple highway intersection or one that's like a cloverleaf. Look at the difference in results. A simple intersection means that some traffic must come to a full stop while other traffic is permitted to proceed. It is all stop and go; consequently, the flow is severely limited. An intersection can handle only so much traffic and no more.

A cloverleaf, however, changes the situation completely. It doesn't impede the flow. It accommodates and facilitates it. There's no need for some traffic to come to a full stop while other traffic is allowed to go through. Instead, all the traffic from various directions can keep moving, and this means that the volume can be enormously increased.

Apply this to churches and leadership styles. Some church leaders function more as a traffic light or a traffic officer—they stand at the intersection directing traffic, stopping some people while allowing others to proceed. The solution to this bottleneck is simple. Get out of the way! Don't fall into the trap of impeding the ever-enlarging activity and life of your church. Work with an expansive concept in your mind's eye that resembles a cloverleaf, where far more can happen, almost without limit. Then you'll be ready for a vital, growing church!

There's yet another way of looking at the principle involved here. Visualize a graph with a line representing how much depends on you in the management of the affairs of your church. Visualize that while that line may begin, as you begin, at a high point on the left side of the graph, it will go steadily down as it cuts across, reaching the lowest possible level on the right. That's a graphic way of saying that if you're doing your job in the right way, you'll become less and less necessary. Your direct involvement will be progressively reduced, allowing you to focus primarily, if not exclusively, on the few and central things you and you alone must do. In other words, you intentionally spread the work so that others can get in on the fun!

Be a Team Builder

The best example for leadership that I can imagine is the example of the Master himself! Surely if anyone in all human history knew how to launch a movement, Jesus did! Wouldn't you agree? Look at what he produced. His masterful style of leadership should not be missed! If you really want to know how to lead, follow the leader of all time; follow the leader par excellence!

Think about it. Consider how much of Jesus' time and energy was devoted to building his team: first, the twelve—the inner circle of disciples; then the forty, the seventy, and finally, the one-hundred-twenty. When his work on earth was finished, our Lord left a powerful following ready to carry out his ministry and to advance his worldwide mission. His extraordinary style of leadership was paying off!

Note these highly significant, but often ignored, words in Acts 1:15: "And in those days Peter stood up in the midst of the disciples *(altogether the number of names was about a hundred and twenty)*" [italics mine]. That's what our Lord had built up for that day when he would turn over the work to others and to the Holy Spirit. If anyone knew what he was doing, Jesus did. He was sharing his dream as he was building his team!

What might we say about Jesus' leadership style? How did he go about exercising his leadership among his ever-increasing following? I submit that his style was that of a good coach. He didn't set out to do it all. He didn't intend to make all the moves, handle all the plays, play the whole game alone. He had no intention of monopolizing the situation.

That is the way I've tried to see my own ministry. I'm not a general leading troops into battle (even though there's a great battle going on). I'm not the CEO managing the entire enterprise for the stockholders. I'm not the conductor leading the chorus in song. In each of these, I'd have put myself up front as the dominating and central figure. No, I'm simply the coach, and if I'm a good coach, I'm attempting to build a worthy team. It will be the team—not I—who will fulfill the dream and win the game!

The good news is this notion of the leader as a coach, not the central act, is wonderfully liberating. It takes out much of the stress. You become free and more relaxed when you know it doesn't all depend on you alone. You're not the sole performer occupying center stage. You're, in fact, on the sidelines, encouraging the players to give it their best.

I've never known burnout, and I think a major reason for this is I've not fancied myself the sole instrument of what's happening in the churches I serve. Further, and most important, I've felt a strong reliance upon the Lord to show the way and to make things happen. I'm building a team with which to share the dream, by which to advance and fulfill the vision. To accomplish this, there are four crucial steps: identify, recruit, train, and set loose.

Identify Potential Leaders

In order to identify the best possible leaders for your vital, growing church, you need to be intentional. I've often wondered how Jesus went about selecting each of the twelve disciples. What was he looking for—what qualities did he seek? Why did he choose this one or that one? Surely in his immense wisdom he was not going at it willy-nilly. For example, note what he said of Nathanael at their first meeting: "Behold, an Israelite indeed, in whom there is no guile" (John 1:46–48). This soon-to-be disciple was floored! "How do You know me?" Nathanael asked in amazement. Jesus responded, "Before Philip called you, when you were under the fig tree, I saw you." The text implies that Jesus was a good observer. He had taken in quite a bit about Nathanael. Identifying good leaders, those suitable for the mission, is a major challenge. It is key to what can happen in your church.

Now I must make a confession: Discernment, apparently, is a gift I've gratefully received from the Holy Spirit, confirmed by spiritual gifts assessment guides. I've found that I quickly sense things about people, and this has been enormously helpful in my ministry. You may be so blessed, too, and you do need to be as discerning as possible when you identify potential leaders. Pay close attention, do your homework, be open to the Spirit's leading, reflect upon the kind of person you're encountering and whether he or she could or should be a player on your team.

If you're a good coach, you're always on the lookout for talent. You may send out talent scouts to find the people you need. This is a major undertaking for any coach trying to build up a winning team. You know that not everyone will do because not everyone will be a team player. Not everyone will believe in the cause or have the spirit to win. A good coach knows this and is forever searching for the right people for the right positions.

You also need to be sensitive to warning signals of the wrong people. On a few occasions, someone will come on strong or come to you with a heavy spiel. When a new minister begins in a church, often those who crave power will move in upon him quickly. Love these people, but don't be taken in. Be discerning, and above all, be open to the Spirit's counsel.

Recruit Your Leaders

Who plays the role of recruiter? Perhaps you do. Perhaps a nominating committee does. Perhaps in your church, some other process is followed. Perhaps it is a combination of all of these. Whatever, adapt the following guidelines to your situation.

In some instances, I have directly approached people I strongly felt were needed in the leadership ranks—not to appoint them but to prepare them. This was especially true of key positions such as board president or chairpersons of major departments, because for these I needed the best and would seek the best.

I've observed, however, that often church leaders take the easy way. They settle for second best, third best, or worse. They have not set their sights high, or wrongly felt that the best candidates are too busy or can't be bothered with the tasks in mind. Actually, people sense what our standards are, and if they sense they're high, those individuals will be flattered that you felt them worthy or needed. Always go for the best!

I recall speaking to one of the most promising people in my congregation. He was deeply committed, enthusiastic about the church and where it was headed, and an admired and highly positioned executive in a major insurance company. I saw him as one with the potential to be a key leader in our church. I asked him if we could have lunch together some day near his office in the city. I told him that I wanted to share some thoughts with him.

Within a week or so we met at a fine restaurant for lunch. In the course of our meal I shared with him my dreams for our church and why I thought those dreams were possible. He clearly responded to the vision I was presenting. Then I said, "But you know, I need help with this. I can't do it alone. I need the right people helping to make it happen. I need people like you."

This man sensed the direction of my remarks and appeared responsive. I said, "You know, in a year or two, you may be asked to become our board president. We need someone like you for that position. What I'm asking now is this: I know you are a busy person. You have lots of commitments and responsibilities. But if, in a year or two, you're approached for such a position, would you make sure you have your commitments in order so that you can say yes?"

The man reflected for a moment and then indicated that he would. He told me that he would be available if and when the time came, and he gave me his assurance. It was evident he was touched to be approached.

The best leadership needs to be thoughtfully, intentionally, and prayerfully identified, and the best leadership needs to be thoughtfully, intentionally, and prayerfully recruited. You honor people when you do this well.

In most churches a nominating committee plays the key role in recruitment, depending on the local situation. I happen to believe the minister or leader of that congregation needs to be part of the process of selection for the team of which he is the coach. No good coach would agree to being circumvented on that score. Not that the minister needs to dominate or dictate, a clumsy way to go about it, but he should be an active participant when the nominating committee is doing its work.

It's most helpful if the committee, working in the spirit of prayer, fully understands the enormity of its task and works with the right criteria. In our church, the nominating committee adopted a set of criteria that guided its reflections year after year. I composed the criteria and presented them to the committee for reflection and adoption. To this day this is the document the nominating committee follows whenever it meets:

NOMINATING COMMITTEE CRITERIA

Nominating is one of the most important tasks in the life of the church. It will profoundly affect whether the church will continue to be strong and thriving or not. Undertake the task with prayer. Seek God's help and direction. As it has been said: "Action without prayer is arrogance; prayer without action is hypocrisy."

Your search for the right people should be intensive and systematic. Somewhere among the members are outstanding people for the tasks you have in mind. The match should be the best you can make. At least half of those proposed should be newer members in order to assure continued vitality. Ask these questions about each potential leader:

1. What is the nature of the particular position we have in mind for this person?
2. Does the person under consideration for a particular position have the required gifts and skills for the task? If a chairperson of a department, does she or he have administrative skills?
3. Has this person demonstrated a deep Christian faith and commitment?

4. Is the person faithful in church attendance?
5. Does the person practice high Christian stewardship?
6. Does the person share the vision of our church as a great and pacesetting church? Is the person "in tune" with our church as it is today?
7. Does the person have the energy and vitality to serve well, never flagging in zeal?
8. Does the person work well with others; is the person a team player rather than a loner?

Our committee would assemble a large list of names suggested by members, by me, and others. Then the committee would evaluate each person, carefully measuring strengths against the standards set. When the committee had completed its work, it was confident that it had chosen wisely.

Whatever the process followed, a systematic review is essential and will help you make the best and wisest choices. Make no mistake, the quality and dedication of your leaders and whether or not they can work well as a team will largely determine how far your church can go and what it can achieve. It behooves everyone to take this step in the process seriously.

Train Your Leaders

Obviously your leadership people, however chosen, need to be trained for their tasks. They need direction. They need to bring the best possible understanding to their responsibilities. Once again look to the Master coach.

It's clear to me that Jesus was constantly training his disciples. Before he sent them out two by two, he gave them clear instructions, preparing them for the challenge. He was confident they were ready for the assignment. Could you do any less? If leadership is to happen, pastors must show initiative, and not leave things to chance.

How can you do this? For one thing, you can hold a leadership retreat, perhaps as an annual event. Take your key leaders away overnight, somewhere far enough from the home base that they'll not be tempted to slip away or attend to various errands. Bring in outside resources, such as a visionary figure as a key speaker for the event—a person who will stretch the mind and help people think in fresh terms concerning the mission of the church.

The retreat is a splendid opportunity for sharing your vision for your church. In that setting, when people are standing back and looking anew at the cause of Christ and their role in it, you can set forth your dreams and your expectations. The prayer times, the sharing times, the worship times—together with the various interactions of the event—will spark a deeper commitment and a readiness to do great things for the Lord.

Another important way for sharing your vision is to take key leaders to workshops and conferences where they will get exposure to new ideas. In New England, we are blessed by Vision New England's annual congress, held in a large convention center in Boston. I would take as many as possible to that event and let them see what opportunities are all around us.

I would also take them to a national conference such as the Robert Schuller Institute for Successful Church Leadership. In fact, it was important that every minister on the staff attend at least once. I wanted their minds stretched, their standards set high, and their sensitivity to reaching people effectively enhanced. There are any number of such opportunities, such as at the Community Church of Joy in Phoenix, Arizona, or Willow Creek Community Church in South Barrington, Illinois. All such exposures will sharpen awareness and help your leaders catch the same vision you have caught.

One of the most useful and effective techniques for training your leaders is so simple one wonders why more pastors do not do it. I select a book from time to time that I feel all of my top people will find stimulating. It might be George Hunter's *The Church for the Unchurched,* Rick Warren's *The Purpose-Driven Church,* or Stephen Macchia's *Becoming a Healthy Church.* Today I certainly would have them read Lyle Schaller's latest work, *The Very Large Church.*

Whatever the book, I buy ten or more copies and bring them to the church board meeting, placing the books without comment at the center of the table. When we reach the end of the evening's agenda and are about to close, I say something like this: "Brothers and sisters, you are the leaders of this church. Our congregation looks to you for leadership. I know you want to do this well. I have a book here that I believe will help you be the kind of leader you want. There's a copy for everyone so take one and read it within the next two months. Then let's see what we've learned, what new understanding and sense of opportunities lie before us."

One by one, the board members pick up a copy as they leave. By the next meeting I can already sense that what they've read is resonating with them. Within a short time, I hear much of the content of the book echoing in our discussions. This, I discovered, is one of the easiest and most effective ways of getting your leadership up to speed and turned on to the vision. Once they've caught that vision, see how it begins to spread throughout the ranks until more of your people reflect that they know what new and novel thing you and they are doing and being.

These methods mean you don't have to lecture or harangue your people as you attempt to share the vision. You will, of course, lift up key ideas from time to time in your preaching, in newsletters, comments, and sharing at board and committee meetings. But so much of this will happen beyond you, with more and more of your leaders articulating what your church is becoming.

No doubt, there are other good ways to train your leaders. The rich offerings in Bible study, small group ministry, and other programs in the life of the church will enhance the quality of leadership. But these methods can be attempted in any church and will assuredly produce wonderful fruit. The quality of leadership will get better and better until it becomes—may I say it?—stunning! You'll often find that your leaders are ahead of you and you need to catch up.

Set Your Leaders Loose

You've come this far. Now dare to believe in your people, leaders, and the larger family of faith. Your efforts will be multiplied many times over as your people run with the vision and live out the dream. This, after all, is what you wanted in the first place. The players are in the field and ready to go. They're truly expressing the priesthood of all believers. You, as a good coach, can from the sidelines watch them play the game to win.

Return again to the example of our Lord. "And He called the twelve to Himself, and began to send them out two by two, and gave them power over unclean spirits" (Mark 6:7).

That was what Jesus had intended. That was what he had in mind when he chose those disciples, when he called them to be with him, when he taught and counseled them along the way. At last, they were ready to go forth to proclaim the kingdom and to expand his ministry. He set them loose!

That is the only way you can undertake and succeed in an expansive and ever-enlarging ministry. You can't do it alone, remember? You can't work at an intersection. You need to multiply the scope of ministry and mission, do your part and then get out of the way, allowing more and more people to experience the joy of ministry. If you're insecure with this, if you feel threatened unless you keep a lid on things, controlling everything that happens, people can't help expand the vison. But if you've done your part, if you trust your leaders, and above all, trust the Spirit of Christ working in and through them, great things will happen. You will be astonished, and you'll have a church ready to take on the world.

Now, regarding recruiting and assigning professional staff: Needs differ between churches depending on size, location, tradition, and the special blend of ministry being provided. Churches today are finding a variety of needs and solutions so that creativity and good analysis are in order.

Some churches recruit from outside, and some find it desirable to recruit from within. One of the best people I ever had on my staff was a woman in our congregation who came on board, picked up the necessary on-the-job training at a nearby seminary, and soon became a superstar performer. The advantage with this approach is that the local person knows the local people and also knows the unique vision of your church. You don't need to wait two or three years for the new person to catch onto what your church is really like, or to learn the ropes.

When bringing in someone from outside, I'd reach out as far as possible, making the position opening widely known and thus initiate a thorough selection process. As the coach, I'd play a close, though not dominating, role. It's good to have the collective wisdom of several good people. The criteria used by the nominating committee would be useful in this selection process too. In the end, I'd want to make sure this staff person understood and enthusiastically embraced the vision of the church.

A recent e-publication of Leadership Network touched upon the fluid state of things in staffing these days. "A variety of new church staff positions are emerging such as stewardship pastor, chief financial officer, minister of technology, webmaster, and graphic artist while other existing positions are being re-framed such as minister of Christian education becoming minister of leadership development and learning."[1] The point is, each church must analyze its needs in terms of its own situation and the most promising way of providing vital leadership.

These leadership style considerations are the heart and soul of effective leadership, of building a great church, and of sharing the dream and building the team!

7

Feed the Sheep, Feed the Lambs

One of the most plaintive passages in the four Gospel accounts is found in John 21, beginning with verse 15. It is Jesus' insistent and last appeal to Peter. I believe our Lord meant this for Peter and all of the disciples, but equally for all of us who would represent the cause of Christ. It's to be the measure of our love for him.

"Do you love Me?" Jesus asked Peter. Receiving an affirmative answer, he said, "Feed My sheep."

A second time he asked, "Do you love Me?" Then, again, "Feed My lambs."

Yet a third time Jesus posed the question as though to leave no doubt as to what he was asking and what he was expecting. To the reply of assurance, he responded, "Feed My lambs!" There's no directive more pertinent to the churches and church leaders today, I believe, than this one.

If you confront the truth, you'll acknowledge that what people find in too many churches is meager fare at best. Sunday after Sunday, week after week, people come and go but don't get fed. The food is bland and unexciting. The sheep go away hungry for spiritual truth. Many don't return; they decide they can spend their time more profitably doing something else. Many decide to look elsewhere for life's answers and for nourishment.

Oh, the churches may go through the paces. Services are held. Sermons are preached. Programs and classes are conducted. But when you stand back and ask, "What are the people getting out of all this?" the honest answer in many instances is "Nothing!" People are simply "doing church," as the expression goes. Should we be surprised, then, if such churches stand still or decline, show little or no forward thrust and a minimal sense of mission?

If there is a compelling dream or a daring and ambitious vision flowing through the life of a church and its leaders, of one thing you can be sure: Those churches will feed people! They will provide sustenance week after week. They will take to heart Jesus' final words to Peter, to the disciples, and to us—to feed the sheep, feed the lambs. Where people are fed, things happen, and the response will be reflected in increasing numbers coming to church.

Many years ago I was asked to consider a call to a church in California. I flew across the country and visited, spent some time with its leadership, then returned, only to conclude the Lord was not calling me there. Some years later, a couple who had been active in that church visited our town in Connecticut, and dropped by the church office.

I enjoyed renewing their acquaintance, then asked how their church was doing. They responded, somewhat sheepishly, that they didn't attend there anymore, but were now actively involved in another church.

They told me that though they both had held key positions in their church (one was superintendent of the church school and the other chaired a committee), one Sunday they asked themselves, "What are we getting out of church? What is there to feed our souls?" They told me, "We went every week. We did our part, but we came away, Sunday after Sunday, empty and unfulfilled. We decided there was no point simply going through the motions, and we went searching for a church where we would be fed."

Feed the sheep! Feed the lambs! Don't waste people's time simply going through motions and "doing church"!

There are four key areas where a vital and growing church will feed people: relevant preaching, exciting worship, the intimacy of small group ministry, and the challenging opportunity for hands-on mission and service. All four of these are important in the life of a great church, and all are important if people are to be fed. Look at each one:

Key 1: Relevant Preaching

Whether we like it or not, in all great movements there's an effective communicator at the center. Whether we like it or not, churches and ministries are generally evaluated in terms of the quality and effectiveness of the preaching. Here's our greatest chance to proclaim the Word of hope and faith to the greatest number of people. Preaching deserves our best and should be among our highest priorities in time and preparation. Fail in communicating the Word, and little is likely to happen. Succeed, and something awesome will happen. Preaching is our first and foremost opportunity to feed the sheep.

Some pastors might dismiss this, thinking not much hinges on what happens in the pulpit or on the platform in the preaching of the Word. Others would prefer to wing it or leave it to the Holy Spirit to make up for their deficiencies and neglect.

One minister liked to say, "I don't spend time on preparation. I just wait for the Holy Spirit to speak to me and to tell me what to say." So he took no pains to prepare. An older and wiser minister responded to him, "I did that once, and the Spirit did speak to me one Sunday. He spoke to me loud and clear, right there in the pulpit, right after my sermon. He said, 'Jones, you're lazy!'"

The awesome responsibility to proclaim the Word of God with all the power at your command is mighty. The awesome privilege of standing before a gathering of people, however few or many, to speak in the name of Christ demands your best, but it's sacrilege to make light of this or to do it poorly through neglect.

I'm not here to present a course on preaching, but a few things do need to be said in this context: A preacher needs to be relevant to people's lives, to their place on the Christian journey, and needs to take aim at the target—the world from which people come.

For one thing, the title of a sermon or a message should be such that people want to hear what's said. Certain titles might just as well be a number—Sermon 1, Sermon 2, Sermon 3—for all the interest they ignite. They may be little more than a tag, meaningful only to the preacher. If so, you'll miss an opportunity to create a compelling itch that people need to scratch. Rick Warren lays it out:

If you scan the church page of your Saturday newspaper, you'll see that most pastors are not attempting to attract the unchurched with their sermon titles. A sample of intriguing sermon topics from the *Los Angeles Times* includes: "The Gathering Storm," "On the Road to Jericho," "Peter Goes Fishing," "A Mighty Fortress," "Walking Instructions," "Becoming a Titus," "No Such Thing as a Rubber Clock," "River of Blood," and "The Ministry of Cracked Pots."

Do any of these titles make you want to hop out of bed and rush to church? Would any of them appeal to the unchurched person scanning the paper? What are preachers thinking? Why are they wasting money advertising titles like these?[1]

So if your preaching is to be relevant to people's lives, deal with issues that are real and important to them. Develop titles that make people say, "I must hear that!" Does this mean watering down the gospel or neglecting the great issues and themes of the Word? Not in the least! It means giving thought to how to reach people, proclaiming the Word so it's clearly important and relevant, and connects.

In his superb book, *How to Reach Secular People,* George Hunter understands this. He graciously cites some titles of mine and says they address "some of the very questions about God that secular searching people most often pose—such as 'Does God exist?' 'What is God like?' 'Can we know God?' 'Does God know us?' 'Is God involved with us?' and 'Can we believe in miracles in a scientific age?'"[2] If the titles do what Hunter says, then I'm happy, because that was what I intended.

One of the most helpful practices I fell into as a pastor was to enlist an official critic. It began thirty years ago when I was young and relatively new in the ministry. I had in my congregation an older retired man who had been in the ministry himself, then left to work in the movie industry in Hollywood. He was a committed Christian and savvy about communication in the modern world.

One day I said to him, "I have a job for you. I want you to be my official but confidential critic." I might have said "coach." Then I explained: "I want you to feel free at all times to tell me what you think I need to be told in order to be more effective in my preaching and leadership in this church. No one will know of this special assignment, but you're always to level with me and tell me what I need to be told."

He did!

He was enormously helpful. Sunday after Sunday, he would speak to me on the side and give me his appraisal. I listened and refused to get defensive. I listened for my own good and the good of those I was trying to serve. When the sermon was good or very good, he would say, "That was a sockdolager!" (Look up that word—I had to.) Then I knew I'd hit a home run. When it was mediocre, he would say so. When I'd missed the boat entirely, he would let me know.

Once I announced a series of Lenten sermons based on our denomination's latest statement of faith. It went like this: "God Acts," "God Creates," "God Judges," "God Comes," "God Renews," "God Calls," and "God Promises." When I composed those titles, I thought they were great. They sounded like solid theology to me. But when my friend and critic saw them, he told me flat out, "I'm bored! I have no interest in hearing those—God this, God that—Oh, God!" He wasn't being irreverent, just making a point. But I was stunned, though I learned my lesson.

Because some titles or themes satisfy your professional or theological taste does not mean they'll do the job where people are. Because some books seem as though they contain solid teaching doesn't mean they'll connect or reach the unreached. Get out of your self-centered rut, was the message from my critic and coach. Focus on people where they are and on what will strike them as relevant. I've been forever grateful for the frank comments of my critic friend.

Since then I've almost always had an official confidential critic. In my most recent ministry, I selected a fine younger man in the field of television with a master's degree in communication. Happily, he was a solid church member and had considered the ministry himself; in time, he became a deacon in the church.

Early on I invited him to my study and gave him the assignment. "You'll be my critic," I said, explaining what I meant. He cheerfully accepted and thereafter helped me tremendously. He brought to my attention things about my preaching, and helped me prepare for television interviews—coaching me on things in which he was the expert. He knew his stuff, I needed and wanted his help, and I remain forever grateful.

The Fuqua International School of Christian Communications at the Crystal Cathedral encourages coaching. It makes one of its prime recommendations to those who take advantage of its excellent program: Get yourself a coach. Some of the greatest and most experienced singers in the world still have a coach, it's pointed out; it doesn't matter how long they have been at it or how old they may be. Others in related fields have a coach, and truly creative people are always learning and always willing to learn from others. Likewise, preachers should have someone who will tell them what they need to hear, whether they like it or not.

As you consider effective preaching, you could hardly do better than to look at the best model of a communicator, the Lord Christ Jesus. If anyone knew how to connect with people, he did. If anyone knew how to be relevant to people and their lives, he did. In the Gospel of John, the fourth chapter, remember the striking and instructive example of how to communicate well with people out there?

Jesus and the disciples are traveling through Samaria when Jesus stops at Jacob's well. Why he stopped at the well is not stated, though you could assume that he wanted water. I think there was another reason. He knew this was a public and central place; sooner or later one person or another would stop to get water. It was a strategic location for communicating the Good News and being heard.

Sure enough, along comes this Samaritan woman. Jesus says, "Give Me a drink." This is an astonishing development, as she is a Samaritan, and Jews have no dealings with Samaritans. Also she is a woman, and this man has broken a barrier between men and women by speaking to her. This is startling. Right away, she is listening. This stranger is connecting with her!

Then the conversation takes a surprising turn. Jesus begins to speak of living water—an appropriate theme as they stood by the well. Notice Jesus did not begin talking theology. He didn't begin lecturing about Scripture. He didn't pull out all the stops for doctrinal accuracy. He spoke of something as basic and necessary to life as water, but more specifically water that would forever quench her deepest thirst. Now this woman is paying attention! Now she's really interested!

Just then, Jesus gives the conversation another significant turn. When the woman asks him to give her this living water "springing up into everlasting life," Jesus asks about her husband. This touches upon her life in a personal way. She acknowledges that she has no husband. In fact, as Jesus points out, she's had five, and is living now with a man who's not her husband.

Jesus continues to draw out who she is, to fascinate her, and to share his message. When she confesses that he must be a prophet to know all this about her, she makes reference to a view associated with the Jews as opposed to the Samaritans. It's only in Jerusalem that God may be worshiped. To this, Jesus makes his most astonishing and revolutionary statement: "The true worshipers will worship the Father in spirit and truth; for the Father is seeking such to worship Him. God is Spirit, and those who worship Him must worship in spirit and truth" (John 4:23–24). How's that for a climax to his message?

Now the woman acknowledges something of her faith: "I know that the Messiah is coming. . . ."

To this, Jesus responds, "I who speak to you am He."

Notice how skillfully Jesus has led to that conclusion and announcement. What began as a seeming chance and casual encounter has become a life-changing event. The woman is overcome. She drops her water pitcher and runs into the city, proclaiming for all to hear, "Come, see a Man who told me all things that I ever did. Could this be the Christ?" Her life would never be the same. Not only that, through her and her witness, we're told many more believed.

Another telling feature in the account as given in the Gospel of John is Jesus' comment to his disciples. Be sure to notice it and consider what it implies: "Behold, I say to you, lift up your eyes and look at the fields, for they are already white for harvest!" (John 4:35). Surely, it was his way of saying: The world is filled with hungry souls like this woman. Just give them the Word in a way that they can understand and that relates to life right where they are.

In that marvelous and revealing episode, Jesus gives us an extraordinary example of effective preaching. It's life-centered, connects, comes across as relevant, touches people where they are, and can have dramatic, transforming results. Jesus wasn't just giving a sermon with the right text and the right exegesis. He was giving a message for life!

Key 2: Exciting Worship

There is in every human heart a desire to experience exaltation, to be lifted up spiritually, and relate to something higher and more wonderful than anything in mundane and everyday affairs. The yearning is to connect with the one from whom all things come—to connect with God! If you are to feed people—the sheep as Jesus commanded—the lambs need the opportunity to enter into a worship that's powerful, lifting, and relevant to their lives.

But is this what most find in their churches? Or is worship more like repeating the right words, singing the right songs, going through the right motions? How can anyone come into the presence of God and not be moved? How can anyone experience the Holy Spirit of God and not feel it's the most exciting time imaginable? To me, the Sunday service offered in many churches should be the high point of the entire week for people—their most exciting hour. Otherwise, we fail our Lord.

You know the famous story of Calvin Coolidge? He went to church one Sunday and, upon his return, was questioned by his wife, Grace. "What did the preacher talk about?"

"He talked about sin," Coolidge answered.

"What did he say about it?"

"He said he was against it."

It's a cute story, but isn't it typical of morning worship in the house of God? Do you honor God when you make worship routine and dull? Are you connecting with God if nothing happens in the minds, hearts, and souls of the people who attend your service?

With the many exciting offerings of entertainment provided in our world today, why should anyone choose to go to church except out of habit and compulsion? If the world can make so exciting what, in fact, is pretty shallow or inconsequential, how can you who love the Lord and believe in the gospel, be content to conduct worship unworthy of your highest, that people can just write off?

Wake up, friends! God deserves your creative best. God deserves far more than you've been content to provide. And if the churches are not to lose ground, however slowly but steadily, many of us better do a better job. Make sure your worship is truly and authentically the happy hour and that church is truly the exciting place to be on Sunday mornings.

Now, I must confess I'm by background and nature a traditionalist. I honor and respect worship as it has been done in the past. I love classical music and enjoy the old hymns. But I've had to face the truth that what's satisfying to me may not be satisfying to increasing numbers of people. The worship needs to be for the sheep, not for me.

Worship needs to be relevant to the times too. It needs to be in keeping with the ways of contemporary people. This doesn't mean that anything goes, nor that pastors should, as some accuse, "dumb down" worship. This, I deeply believe, is not necessary for worship to connect with people. On the other hand, let it also be said that worship isn't the exclusive domain of the elite, those fastidious folk quite sure of what the liturgy should be—wholly focused on God to the neglect of people. After all, the message of the incarnation, the central miracle of faith, is that God humbled himself and came down, taking on human flesh to dwell among people, to be one with us. Some might say that in so doing God was dumbing down to the human level.

If there was anything about Jesus that set him apart to people, though, it was that "this Man spoke as no man spoke" and "the common people heard Him gladly" (Mark 12:37). If we follow his example out of our concern for people, it seems pastors should be on guard against the legalism and the exclusivity Jesus so clearly abhorred. Our Lord would want his people to speak to others in ways they understand, to conduct worship in ways that engage them, to connect with people in all walks of life. This is no time to restore the temple veil, which in effect says, "Stand back, keep your distance, God is too holy for you!"

Worship may well be shaped by the heritage and setting where you find yourself, and the particular people you're trying to reach. This may mean that you move toward the traditional forms that are yet vibrant and meaningful. Or it may mean you move toward the contemporary styles appreciated by our younger generation. Or it may be a blending of both. Each pastor must judge his or her own situation and decide what's the best approach.

In our historic Connecticut church, the main Sunday morning services are a blend of both, following the traditional pattern but containing much that would be called contemporary. Other worship opportunities are also provided, some of an even more contemporary style and some of a charismatic style. A full-service church will make various choices available so that nearly everyone will find something to relate to in the experience of worship.

How can you make your worship relevant and exciting so that people are fed? As the psalmist put it, "I was glad when they said to me, 'Let us go into the house of the LORD'" (Ps. 122:1). Surely such joy and gladness ought to be replicated in your time and church. Consider these nine ways:

Clearly Focus on God

Bring glory to God and glorify his name. People sense when worship is authentic, and they'll respond to it, provided it's done in such a way as not to obscure the glorious presence of God. In my call to worship, I often use the magnificent words from the shorter catechism of the Westminster Confession with a slight modification. "What is the chief purpose of life?" I ask. To that the people respond, "To glorify God and to enjoy Him forever." It's a stirring way to begin worship, and it clearly indicates focus.

Express Joy in the Presence of God

The worship leader sets the tone by voice, manner, and facial expression. Joy will be contagious. More and more people will feel it and respond to it. Solemn faces may be appropriate at certain times, but not for typical Sunday worship.

Exude Warmth and Intimacy

Worship is corporate, not a private meditation. Together in the presence of God there should be interaction. How the service is opened and the first words spoken will shape the atmosphere. For this reason I prefer to begin by standing close to the people where they connect with me and I connect with them. I choose not to stand behind the pulpit, lectern, or some other barrier. If I exude warmth, they return warmth and feel welcomed—and welcoming.

My first words may be a simple "good morning." The congregation responds, "Good morning." Then I say, "Welcome to First Church, where the Spirit is alive and where miracles happen. What a beautiful morning we shall have in this place! But first, let us take a moment to greet and welcome one another."

It's important at the very outset of the service for people to greet one another, relate to those around them, and experience togetherness. The ice is broken at the earliest possible moment. I don't wait until halfway through the service or the close for such mutual greetings. The people need it at the beginning so that right away they feel that they're among friends.

Having allowed a few moments—not too long—for this exchange, I pick it up and signal the start of worship with something like this: "I was glad when they said unto me, 'Let us go into the house of the Lord.'" Or, "This is the day the Lord has made; let us rejoice and be glad in it." Or, "Come into the circle of love and justice. Come into the fellowship of pity, holiness, and health. Come, and you shall know peace and joy." At once, the choral introit bursts forth, followed by the opening hymn.

Many pastors would have an announcement period at this point. I choose not to, preferring that later. To me, coming into God's house should be so thrilling that one cannot delay long in singing for joy and magnifying God. As soon as possible we should be focusing on him. If I were led into the king's chambers, I couldn't stand around talking about pedestrian matters. I'd quickly, be on my knees before his Majesty! Let the other stuff wait.

Move and Progress

The pacing of a service has become critical today because people are conditioned by television where the pacing is rapid and no dead spots are permitted. Hence, the attention span is shortened. You may regret and deplore that, but that's the way it is, folks. So pokey worship, long waiting between each segment with a delay of ten seconds or more, suggests dullness and dreariness. In fact, that kind of service will be perceived as lacking energy. The service should move! Worship leaders shouldn't sit in their seats until the preceding agenda item is over. If one is to read Scripture, one should be in place and ready to do it the moment the last thing is finished. I timed my associates and they soon became conscious of the dead spaces created by lagging.

Prayers also shouldn't exceed a certain span of time, say four or five minutes at the most. The Scripture lessons shouldn't be more than a certain number of verses, let's say ten or fifteen; the morning message shouldn't be more than twenty-two minutes. Self-discipline by staff means the service is far more likely to provide exciting, not boring, worship.

Provide Sharing of Faith and Testimony

Halfway through our service we have what we call "a moment of fellowship." This is sort of a good seventh-inning stretch, helping people to take a breath before moving into the second half. It's also a time for necessary announcements and a mystery guest—an unannounced visitor as on the TV program *The Hour of Power.* In this way we include in the service testimonies, faith-sharing, and hearing from someone other than the preacher. These are powerful times and present a modern form of the old-time testimonies, which from New Testament times were important for sharing "what God is doing in my life." They also give a service an element of surprise and spontaneity.

Enhance Worship with Modern Devices

This entails the use of overhead projectors or TV screens, bringing the elements closer, especially in a large sanctuary or meeting hall. These devices also provide a unifying effect, with everyone seeing the same words together. Some churches will project the Scriptures, main points of the message, or other information for helpful reinforcement. In today's world people are accustomed to all sorts of devices that help them in their comprehension and bring a certain immediacy. Provided multimedia is used well, and not distracting, it can contribute to the excitement and liveliness of worship.

Of course there will always be people who resent technical devices in the house of God, so exercise discretion, but know this resentment of such new-fangled ways is age-old. A church I once served in Litchfield, Connecticut, provided a wonderful illustration of this reluctance. Apparently, back in the early 1800s, it was proposed that the church be heated by installing a wood burner. This was scandalous to some, who fought it tooth and nail. True worship should be in the cold! Only gradually was the idea accepted. Happily, during my time at that church, we had central heating, and nobody complained or called it sacrilegious.

Incorporate Drama

Many churches with contemporary worship use a brief segment of drama to highlight the theme of the message. It often effectively brings home an issue, helping people sense the relevance of the theme. If Jesus taught in parables, drama can serve as the parabolic aspect of the service. People are captivated, intrigued, and focused for what will follow.

In our contemporary church services, we use drama regularly; at our Sunday morning services we frequently use puppets, all beautifully staged. In fact, our puppet ministry has become an important aspect of our church life.

Be Rich with Music

Music may be familiar, traditional, classical, or contemporary. I feel every service should include one magnificent traditional piece and something that really touches people today in a relevant way. That's because at least half of the delight and power of a service is through its music. In our church, the music was meager and remote when I began. We've since brought in people who have made it spectacular.

Provide Clues

When people come into your church the first time, they know little of what you represent. Thoughtful fashioning of the service bulletin can help enormously. It should say something about your congregation and its atmosphere.

Simply listing the name of the church and the elements of service won't do. In a prominent location in our Sunday morning bulletin, we wrote:

Welcome!
Thank You for Worshiping with Us!
Welcome to First Church, dating from 1635, and worshiping in this Meetinghouse erected in 1761. We are the largest and one of the most vital Congregational Churches in New England. We welcome all who seek faith, hope and joy, and for whom Christ is the Lord of Life. Find here an accepting, caring, nonjudgmental spirit where lives are transformed, faith is renewed, and power for positive living is found. God loves you and so do we!

From this bulletin, people who were new in our midst could get a sense of where we were coming from and where we were headed. Thought was given as to what signals we gave people who came into our congregation, too. We asked, "Are those signals inviting, reassuring, caring, and clearly in the name of Jesus Christ?"

Key 3: Intimacy of the Small Group Ministry

Preaching and worship, when large numbers of people gather and celebrate God, are valuable and important, but they don't fulfill all the needs of the seeker or the faithful. The interior life of the church, then, must be rich, fulfilling, and ever expanding. Here's where a variety of programs and groups are needed, and small group ministry becomes indispensable.

A bare-bones church life will not do. A church that provides little more than Sunday morning worship is not doing its job either. Worship is important, in fact, central to the life of a church and to the life of the believer. But other needs must be met if people are to be fed, nurtured in the faith, and growing in grace. The intimacy of close community is essential.

Early on in our church we began addressing this need. An associate minister on the staff was given a new designation: associate minister for parish development. His job was to initiate various groups and programs as the need arose. The first need identified and addressed was the growing population of singles. I'd attended a nonchurch conference on singles (mainly attended by psychologists, counselors, and social workers), where it was announced that within two years half of the adult population would be single—divorced, widowed, never married, or not yet married. Immediately it registered with me: "My church will be irrelevant to half the adult population!" So our church began a singles ministry that started modestly and grew until hundreds were regularly attending. In fact, ours became the leading singles ministry in the state, drawing people to our church who had no church connection or a nominal one. In time, many of these people found their way to becoming church members, some of our most committed.

Other groups were formed: Koinonia, Bible study, mothers, divorce recovery, grief recovery group, and others with the expanding music ministry. This meant people could connect in a more personal way, form closer relationships, and feel more genuinely part of the church. It meant deeply felt needs were being met. It also meant that people found themselves growing in their faith and growing in grace. But these new entities were only the beginning, and in time we lost count of how many groups and programs were being provided. More recently, yet more groups have come into being, such as our men's ministry, seniors ministry, the Alpha program, and others.

Small group ministry of a deliberate and intentional form is the mark of great and growing churches. People need the large celebration times of worship, but they also need smaller units where they can connect with individuals and be personally supported in their faith. Various models have come into being in recent years, some working well in new churches, others working well in older, established churches. Each group must fit the situation.

Of course, this is the sort of thing that went on in the early church when house churches were everywhere. In the writings of Paul, for example, there are repeated references to "the church in your house" or "in his house" or "in their house" (Rom. 16:5; 1 Cor. 16:19). These were small group ministries at their best. Shouldn't any church in our day desiring to be an "apostolic" church take note of this New Testament model?

David Yonggi Cho of Seoul, Korea, set the pace on this. In 1981 he published his book *Successful Home Cell Groups,* describing how he began to build an extraordinary church wholly based on small group ministry. Cells, as they were called, multiplied as more and more people were nurtured in that closely connected setting. The church consequently grew at a phenomenal rate, reaching a membership of eight hundred thousand.

Other notable churches have adopted the small group ministry model. Each has its own special character and procedure, but all look to lay leadership—a key aspect— to make it happen. Dale Galloway, then pastor of New Hope Community Church in Portland, Oregon, pioneered in this, developing more than six hundred "Tender Loving Care" (TLC) groups. Rick Warren has used small group ministry as one strategy for the growth of his purpose-driven Saddleback Valley Community Church. Similarly,

Bill Hybels has incorporated small group ministry into the life of Willow Creek Community Church. All of these are amply and expansively described in George G. Hunter's most helpful book *Church for the Unchurched.*

Vision New England, the "Movement of Hope" working with and through more than one thousand New England churches, has rightly identified the importance of this aspect of church life and development. To that end, it's taken on its excellent and dedicated staff an expert in the field, Diana C. Bennett, to counsel and help equip the churches of New England in small group ministry.

Bennett has described the nature of this ministry:

> Large and small churches alike struggle with the lack of close-
> ness and fellowship that Christ intends for us to share in his
> body. The small group ministry, when understood and well
> led, fulfills that void in a powerful way. Creating groups of
> 10–12 people who meet on a regular basis, caring for one
> another, praying and worshipping the Lord together, encour-
> aging each other to grow in their relationships with one
> another and with Christ, develop disciples who mature in
> their spiritual lives and become witnesses to others.[3]

Whatever the particular formula or model adopted, rich-
ness of programs and small group ministry are essential elements in a vital, growing church meeting the needs of the times and fulfilling the mission of Christ.

Key 4: Hands-on Mission and Service

Is it enough simply to enjoy relevant preaching, experi-
ence exciting worship, or simply to share in the intimacy of small group ministry? Hardly!

This fourth, altogether necessary aspect of feeding the sheep, feeding the lambs is mission and service. You have to do something with, and for, the faith. Act upon it. Go forth in some meaningful way for Christ. This will confirm your discipleship and provide the means for your deepest fulfillment.

In our church more and more people matured in faith and undertook some form of mission or service. It happened with ever-increasing frequency, and was astonishing, a delight to behold as young and old became involved in some expression of Christ's love for humanity. A kind of chain reaction challenged members of the congregation to go out to share with others the love of Christ.

Some people became active in prison ministry. Some volunteered time at a shelter for the homeless. Others helped with our Sidewalk Sunday School in the inner city after the pattern of Bill Wilson's Metro Ministry, or spent long hours and days with Habitat for Humanity, building houses for the poor. Many made major commitments to overseas mission—short-term or longer.

It was thrilling to see a veritable explosion of our people getting involved, making a commitment, serving Christ, and witnessing about him—astounding, in fact. We weren't pushing these things. We simply let people know what opportunities there were, and their heightened sense of divine calling sent them on their way.

Even as I write these words, a young woman from our church is returning from a mission trip to Africa. This morning I prayed for her safe return. Out of college only a few years ago, she evidences a beautiful passion to serve our Lord. This recent trip is but one of her involvements in mission and service. But she is not alone. There are many more like her, and they were nurtured in a church where mission and service were acknowledged as an essential part of its life and message.

The point here is that relevant preaching deserves your best, exciting worship is important and should bring glory to God, and small group ministry is essential for people to connect with others on faith's journey, but there's more to what the church should be about. Remembering our Lord's words, "Go forth and make disciples," your people must go forth in service and mission. A vital and growing church will make this a major aspect of its life and purpose. Feed the sheep, feed the lambs, and amazing and beautiful things will happen!

8

Let Your Light Shine

Now, suppose you're empowering your people, thinking creatively, casting your vision, meeting people where they are, leading with style, and feeding your congregation. What then? What is yet another thing that deserves and requires your attention? There's a clue in Jesus' words from the Sermon on the Mount: "You are the light of the world. A city that is set on a hill cannot be hidden. Nor do they light a lamp and put it under a basket. . . . Let your light so shine before men, that they may see your good works and glorify your Father in heaven" (Matt. 5:14–16).

So there you have it, straight from our Lord, "Let your light shine!" Be visible. Let others see and know what good things are happening. Don't hide these things, whether intentionally, through neglect, or false humility. Get out the message. Project an inviting image. Communicate to the world all around you what you are about and why they should be a part of it. In so doing, you bring glory to God!

Do all churches let their light shine? Do they give thought to how to come across to people in the world?

Or is it too easily and unwisely assumed that if a church just tends to its business, others will know about it and come? Many churches seem to assume this will just happen. But does it? Think of the vast amounts of money spent—some observers say at least 5 percent of the budget expended by businesses is to advertise their product or service. Corporations have no illusions that they can do business without advertising. If they did, they would quickly learn otherwise. Before World War 1, a certain well-known brand of soap was the No. 1 bestseller nationwide. Then for a couple of years during the war, the company stopped advertising. Soon after the war, that well-known brand was gone and its company out of business!

To the extent that a church has visibility—and visibility is the issue here—what kind of image is projected? Is it tediously churchy at best? Is it the same old stuff? A turn-off? Let it be said that the kind of image many, if not most, churches project is not only dull, but a disservice to the cause of Christ!

Go back to our Lord's command: "Let your light so shine before men, that they may see your good works and glorify your Father in heaven." That's not a suggestion. It's a command from our boss, intended for us to make good on it. Pay some attention to public relations. Project the most positive and inviting image to as many people as possible, as far as possible, for the good of the cause and to build up the body of Christ!

Creative Communication

What kind of business are you in anyway? Well, you could say you're mainly in the communication business. Churches are called to communicate the Good News, to "go forth and make disciples." Now going forth can be done in a number of ways. The main thing is to get out the Word. Reach into the world with a compelling message. Ask yourself whether you're giving this aspect of your church real thought and attention. Are you doing it well—creatively, imaginatively, and successfully?

Reading the latest pictorial directory of my church in Connecticut, I noted my successor's timely words in the introduction: "Dear Members and Friends of First Church, Communication, communication, communication! These are the watchwords of our day and age. With good communication, First Church grows closer to our Lord, to each other and to fulfilling our mission. Without it, we would miss out."

Exactly! We in the church are in the business of communication. Therefore, let your light shine!

There's another way of looking at this, taking note of the words and commands of Jesus. "Follow Me," he said, "and I will make you fishers of men" (Matt. 4:19). What a remarkable paradigm! I'm no fisherman, but I do know a few obvious things about successful fishing. For one thing, good fishermen go where the fish are; they don't wait for fish to come to them. You go out to fish, not in places where no fish are to be found. You go where they are— extend yourself into the world of the fish! Next, fish don't bite all the time, only when they're hungry and the water's in the state they prefer. So you fish in terms of where the fish are coming from, and when they're ready to bite. Next, use the right hook for the particular fish, not just the kind of hook you happen to like or that might have caught you once upon a time! It's got to be right for the particular fish, neither too large nor too small—just right! Then, to be sure, you need the right bait. You may not like this bait yourself. It may not suit your fancy—worms or whatever may not satisfy your epicurian taste—but you're not fishing to catch yourself. You're fishing for someone else out there. So if you're a good fisherman, you get informed about these things. What will this fish take to, and what might scare the fish?

Don't you suppose something like this is what Jesus had in mind when he said, "I will make you fishers of men"? I believe it was. After all, he knew fishermen. He moved among fishermen. He was calling and recruiting fishermen. Although they did most of their fishing with nets, they knew in a flash what he was getting at. They sensed, no doubt, that he was a successful fisherman too when it came to people.

As in baiting a hook and communicating well, you and your congregation are in sales, unabashedly and unashamedly in sales for the kingdom! The greatest evangelist in America in Colonial times, George Whitefield, was a super salesman for Christ, and he clearly realized it. His skills in this respect have much to do with the astounding effectiveness of his evangelism and why thousands flocked to hear him in whatever city or town he visited. Study his methods. See if it isn't so. For starters, read Yale historian Harry Stout's excellent biography of Whitefield, *The Divine Dramatist*. What if we had more Whitefields, fishermen with his savvy?

This brings to mind one of my favorite responses when the chairpersons of our church worried about the weather on Fair Day. They would ask me if I would assure them of good weather, presuming I possessed such power. Often I would answer, "Sorry, but I'm in sales—not management!" I was, I am, and all of us who labor to spread the Word are in sales.

So, however you express it, our Lord expects you to do a good job of reaching people, whether it's by workable techniques of fishing or by letting your light shine for all to see. The point is unmistakable: We in the church are called to do a first-rate public relations job. We're to do a first-rate communications job, a first-rate sales job, and a first-rate advertising job. These are not to be an after-thought, of marginal consideration, or elective. They're points central to our evangelistic task—if we would make good on the mission committed to us by our Lord Christ.

Effective Advertising

When I began the work in Connecticut, the church was rapidly losing members and declining in worship attend-ance. From my point of view, little was being done to aggressively counter this or communicate beyond the walls of the church.

To be sure, the gorgeous Meetinghouse caught attention because it was such an imposing building. But people eas-ily eyed it with appreciation and then moved on, giving little or no thought to what might be going on inside. Nothing was going forth that said, "Come, see what's hap-pening and join in the fun!" No one was asking, beyond the immediate community, "How visible is our church?"

As you may have guessed, I believe churches should advertise. I believe in doing it well and imaginatively. Further, I believe a church should generously allow for this in its annual budget, as an essential element of an effective movement. However, much to my dismay, I discovered our church had nothing in its budget for this purpose. Somehow the view prevailed that advertising was unnecessary and ineffective, a notion some denominational people at the time seemed to be advancing.

What could I do? I decided on a simple appeal. Since I was the new guy on the block, they might tolerate my making a few strange requests. So at one of my first church board meetings, I told the board that I believed the church should get the word out, that some degree of advertising was desirable, and that I needed funds to get it started. "Humor me," I said, "and give me five hundred dollars for this purpose!" They did. No questions asked. That meant for the last few months of the budget year I had enough money to begin running ads in the city newspaper.

It seemed pointless—in fact, disruptive and ineffective—to engage in a debate on the worth of advertising or the philosophy behind it. I realize in some parts of the country, church advertising is an accepted and widely practiced thing. But this was New England, and a certain corner where few churches would do something considered this "crass."

Our church was breaking new ground. We launched our advertising program, and it became a regular feature of the Saturday edition of the newspaper. Different locations tend to catch the eye of different people, so sometimes we would place it on the so-called church page, and other times on the TV page or entertainment section.

A funny thing happened in the next few years. Other churches began advertising. In fact, most of them began doing so. Not only that, some began to copy our designs, so we had to keep changing our ads so they wouldn't get lost. We were reminded, "Imitation is the best form of flattery."

In designing a church ad, it's not enough to give the name and address of the church with pertinent information about times of services. Most church names don't convey much. They don't reveal the spirit, character, or style of a church. So, if you can't change your church name to something that catches attention, I believe in some sort of slogan. We began with this: "First Church of Christ—The Exciting Place on Sunday Mornings." Later we adopted another slogan that became a permanent fixture in the publications and self-identification of the church: "Where the Spirit is Alive and Miracles Happen." This last slogan has many benefits. We carry it in the telephone book Yellow Pages, clarifying who we are as a church.

One day the phone rang at our receptionist's desk, and when she answered it, she heard a woman's voice asking, "Is this the church where the Spirit is alive and miracles happen?"

"Yes, it is," answered the receptionist.

"Well, I need a miracle, and I'll be coming to your church!" She did, and her life was never the same again. She had come through a horrendous time in her life and was desperate for hope. That woman is a part of our church to this day—all because our slogan clicked in her hour of greatest need.

I should point out that our initial slogan, "The Exciting Place on Sunday Mornings," was quickly criticized. At a deacons' meeting soon after the first appearance of our ad, one deacon expressed outrage. It was bad enough that we were advertising, the deacon said, but this slogan, "The Exciting Place on Sunday Morning," was "undignified."

I tried to respond as gently and nondefensively as possible, explaining what we were trying to do. I added that, while it might not be dignified, I recalled how Dwight L. Moody, himself accused of being less than dignified, once noted that "dignity is not listed among the fruits of the Spirit." The deacons determined not to interfere, we went on to other matters, and the issue never came up again.

In our effort to get out the word, we also began running television ads. A TV expert, the same one who was my confidential critic and coach, took on the assignment to put one together, showing people gathered for worship during coffee hour, being greeted, and conveying a happy message with happy people in a happy church. Our expert did the necessary taping, wrote the copy, and intoned the message. Then we signed a contract with our local NBC station, and the thirty-second ad was carried early Sunday mornings following the *Hour of Power.*

Since nothing was in the budget to fund this, I made a direct appeal to twenty or thirty individuals, explaining in a letter what I hoped to do, what it might do for our church, and asking if they would help accomplish it. Most said yes, some declined, and we had the money to go forward.

The initial reaction when the ads were first aired was critical, if not one of shock. "Whoever heard of a church running TV ads?" some asked. This initial criticism did not last, when it was discovered that nearly half of those joining our new member class had come because of the TV ad. We began to include advertising as an item in our regular budget, and quickly it was an accepted feature of our communication outreach.

A word of caution, however. If such television advertising is undertaken, it should be done well. A prominent church in an adjoining city decided to follow our example, hired television people, and put together an ad. The pastor reported to me later that there were no results. Advertising was a total loss, he said, money down the drain! But frankly, the ad their professionals came up with was dull and institutional. It simply showed an empty church and the minister standing on the altar steps. It gave an invitation to attend that church but had none of the aliveness or compelling appeal of our ad. So, if you advertise, make your ad good, winsome, and alive!

In your publicity, give attention to good press releases for local newspapers about exciting events taking place in your church. If you want good press, you need to help make it happen. You need to send in good material on a timely and consistent basis, and respect the journalists and reporters if and when they come by to do a story, too.

We had the best press attention of any church in the entire area because we tried to be helpful and responsive. I suppose also we had more and more interesting, newsworthy things going on, making it increasingly difficult to be ignored. Like Jesus positioning himself at the well of Samaria, we positioned ourselves to be accessible to those who wrote the news.

In fact, there was an established rule. My instructions were, "Any time a reporter calls or comes by, I am available." My secretary knew we didn't put such people on hold, nor try to avoid them. They were simply doing their jobs, and we wanted to help.

Expand Who You Are

We did other things to allow our light to shine brightly and be a city set on a hill. We brought in guest speakers or preachers of note. The earliest was William Stringfellow, widely known in his day, now deceased. Later we had Elton Trueblood as our morning preacher, a notable and marvelous figure, powerfully expressing the Christian faith. Yet another was Bruce Larson, called "The Prophet of Relational Theology" by *Christianity Today* magazine. He elevated our church with a beautiful, engaging message. Then, too, when Robert Schuller came to us, people far and wide took notice, and droves clamored to hear him. Not only did our people benefit from these outstanding communicators of the faith, but the larger area began to perceive our church as one of considerable excitement. We could no longer be ignored. We were enjoying high visibility.

Other elements added to the life of our church. We began a concert series under the able leadership of our minister of music, and these came to be seen as must-attend events. We hosted programs and lectureships. Yale historian Harry Stout was commissioned to give a lecture on Jonathan Edwards, who lived in our community and attended our church during his student days. The event was well publicized and drew a large crowd, adding to the stature of the church.

Our Easter and Christmas Eve services began to draw more and more people. We finally had to hold four services—a full house every time—in order to accommodate everyone. Since it's been found that Christmas Eve provides the best opportunity for reaching the unchurched, we took this into account.

A high point in our increasing visibility came in December 1984, when CBS decided to televise our Christmas Eve candlelight service, live and nationwide. That was really a big time for us, a major production with sophisticated equipment and personnel coming in from New York. The entire service needed to be carefully planned and timed. We were told that thirty million viewers joined us that night in celebrating the birth of Christ.

Admittedly, some may wonder, "How do you get all these things done? Who has the time to cover so much? How can more and more be added to the life of the church?" Remember, any leader or pastor who feels responsible to do or control everything will have a tough time. I suspect this is why many get bogged down and find it difficult to have their church be as creative as possible.

The key is the team! Along with thoughtfully building the professional staff ahead of the growth is bringing more and more people into the act, letting others be a greater part of what's happening. Find ways—and there are good materials available for doing this—of identifying the gifts of people and fitting their gifts to the various forms of service that a thriving church must undertake. As different people can do different things, you'll experience together the joy of being part of a vital, growing church.

Take Inventory Regularly

So how visible has your church become? Is your light shining far and wide? Is the city on a hill being seen and attracting people to a place where they can find faith and find the Lord? Take inventory on a regular basis.

At new member meetings, we regularly distribute a questionnaire to check on ourselves and determine how successful we are in our outreach. We ask:

- How did you first hear about First Church?
- Why did you come the first time?

- Why did you continue to come?
- What's the one thing you most want and look for in your church?

The replies are most helpful, and enable us to keep on course—or get on course. Many testify on how they read something about our church that intrigued them, or saw our TV ad, or read something in the newspaper that compelled them to come and check us out. When they came they weren't disappointed; they found a warm, caring, faith-filled church where Jesus' presence was experienced and his love felt.

Individual testimonies confirmed our efforts. I once asked a new member, a man who came to us from several towns away, "How did you happen to come to First Church?" He responded that he had a growing awareness of our church. He kept hearing things about us, and finally came to see if all he was hearing was true.

"It was!" he added.

Today this man is a vital and helpful part of our church. He became a deacon, and in his professional capacity has provided outstanding service to our church. But none of these things ever would have happened if we had not been carrying on a vigorous program of reaching out and communicating far and wide.

Such is the case with yet another man who lives out of state but was unhappy with his church connections—for good reason, I might add. One Sunday he said to his wife, "Let's try to find that wonderful church we've so often said we'd like to visit." They came, and he told me, "We were enthralled with the service. We were touched with the spirit of worship, and our hearts were wonderfully warmed. We just couldn't help returning for a repeat visit, and before long this became a habit." The message got to him, and today he's helping us enormously. He's on the team, sharing the dream!

The urgency of a church reaching out is made plain by the firm and insightful words of Paul. In Romans 10:13 he states the case emphatically: "For 'whoever calls on the name of the LORD shall be saved.' How then shall they call on Him in whom they have not believed? And how shall they believe in Him of whom they have not heard? And how shall they hear without a preacher? And how shall they preach unless they are sent?"

Paul might have added one more question for today: "And how shall they hear unless the churches reach out, effectively, creatively, and persistently communicating to those on the outside, the untouched and the unsaved?"

The challenge to a vital, growing church is unavoidable: Get the Word out! Let your light shine!

9

Pace the Growth
—and Change

The idea hit me while watching the Olympics: Pacing is crucial. It may determine how well one finishes, whether a contender reaches the finish line, or whether the race can be won. No less is this principle true of leading a church into a mode of dynamic growth and vitality. Here, too, the pacing may make all the difference, for there can be rough, disturbing times, and it's entirely possible that at some critical point the whole effort will explode in your face.

In a significantly changing, rapidly growing church, it shouldn't be surprising, in fact, it may be expected, that some people won't be happy. Some may not like what they perceive to be happening. Others may object outright. Still others may gather around them forces of resistance or simply leave. Maybe these folks don't like change, have other ideas or agendas, or have some sort of personal interest in things as they've been. Maybe they have other loyalties and priorities out of sync with what you appear to be doing or leading. Whatever the reason, they can make things difficult, and become troubling roadblocks to moving ahead into a brighter, more promising future.

Face Opposition with Grace

Often through the years, I've had occasion to reflect on what happened to Jesus. People were coming to him. They were attracted and curious. "What new thing is this?" they no doubt asked each other. They checked out Jesus, listened to what he had to say, and then made up their minds. Some stayed with him while others left, and apparently were not heard from again.

Read that revealing passage in John 6, beginning with verse 59. We are told Jesus was teaching in Capernaum, suggesting his way, telling what he was about, giving some idea of the direction he was moving. But it quickly became clear that some people found his plan difficult to accept. Many of his followers reacted negatively, "This is a hard saying; who can understand it?" they responded. Jesus tried to explain but apparently not to the satisfaction of his questioners or critics.

Read, "From that time many of His disciples went back and walked with Him no more" (John 6:66). Early in his ministry, even our Lord Jesus Christ encountered stiff opposition among would-be followers. He was thwarted and met with resistance. If it could happen to Jesus, why should any Christian be surprised if somewhere along the way something similar happens? Maybe Christians should expect challenges when they do the job, leading the church into a new era.

Take heart, however, from the response of true believers, the true disciples who stood up to the plate. "Then Jesus said to the twelve, 'Do you also want to go away?' But Simon Peter answered Him, 'Lord, to whom shall we go? You have the words of eternal life. Also we have come to believe and know that You are the Christ, the Son of the living God'" (John 6:67–69).

Surely that was a critical moment. The cause was hanging by a thread. But a few disciples came through. A few stayed with him, and caught the vision. A few were ready to keep moving ahead. The movement Jesus launched survived and was on its way to the ultimate fulfillment and victory. Ponder that when and if you find yourself up against opposition or if things seem for a time to be turning against you. "Remember the word that I said to you, 'A servant is not greater than his master'" (John 15:20).

A poem I learned as a young man is relevant here. Any would-be leader ready to take on a big challenge might find something of merit in these lines from Rudyard Kipling's poem "If":

> If you can keep your head when all about you
>   Are losing theirs and blaming it on you,
> If you can trust yourself when all men doubt you,
>   But make allowance for their doubting too;
> If you can wait and not be tired of waiting,
>   Or being lied about, don't deal in lies,
> Or being hated don't give way to hating,
>   And yet don't look too good, nor talk too wise.
>
> If you can dream—and not make dreams your master;
>   If you can think—and not make thoughts your aim,
> If you can meet with Triumph and Disaster
>   And treat those two imposters just the same;
> If you can bear to hear the truth you've spoken

Twisted by knaves to make a trap for fools,
Or watch the things you gave your life to, broken,
     And stoop and build 'em up with worn-out tools.

If you can make one heap of all your winnings
     And risk it on one turn of pitch-and-toss,
And lose, and start again at your beginnings
     And never breathe a word about your loss;
If you can force your heart and nerve and sinew
     To serve your turn long after they are gone,
And so hold on when there is nothing in you
     Except the Will which says to them: "Hold on!"

If you can talk with crowds and keep your virtue,
     Or walk with Kings—nor lose the common touch,
If neither foes nor loving friends can hurt you,
     If all men count with you, but none too much;
If you can fix the unforgiving minute
     With sixty seconds' worth of distance run,
Yours is the Earth and everything that's in it,
     And—which is more—you'll be a Man, my son!

You're Not Alone in Crisis

Some of the most remarkable ministries of our day have experienced trying times. They didn't sail along effortlessly. They weren't always unanimously supported by the people around them. In fact, I've yet to find a single great ministry or a single great example of creative and cutting-edge leadership that didn't have its dark night of the soul. All have paid the price! They all bore their cross!

Take the magnificent Community Church of Joy in Phoenix, led by my good friend and colleague Walt Kallestad. Truly, I find it one of the most thrilling examples of a great church doing remarkable things for the king and the kingdom. But has it always been easy or without pain, cost, or a cross? Hardly! Listen to Kallestad's story:

> In God's great prompting and providence, following my preparation at Luther Seminary, I received a call to Phoenix. It was a dream come true for our family. A fantastic opportunity for mission and ministry was located right on the edge of one of the fastest growing cities in America.
>
> The first Sunday came. My congregation was four years old and had approximately 90 worshipers and 260 members. I gave my first "inspiring" message. Bubbling over, I stood at the door greeting people after the service. One member came up to me with a scowling face and grunted, "Whose side are you on?"
>
> I was taken aback and flippantly responded, "God's side." My questioner stomped off.
>
> The next Sunday I was notified there was a fist fight in the parking lot. Two of my church officers were actually punching it out!
>
> Things got worse. My work was criticized. Several did not like the fact that I wanted the church to grow and reach out. They argued over how much of a raise to give me. It was a mess.
>
> As the weeks passed, the problems grew. . . . The success for the first six months was phenomenal for we "grew" from 260 members to 100. I figured that in about six months we could just close up the place. I was devastated.
>
> One evening when the temperature skyrocketed to 120 degrees, the church caught fire. I rushed to my car and, clutching the steering wheel, I cried, "God, what is wrong? I had this inspired dream of a great church but it's all falling apart. God, I need you. I can't keep on without you. You take charge and if anything great happens, I will give you all the credit. I promise." A ton of weight was lifted from my shoulders in that moment. A new desire and spirit were placed in my heart.
>
> Slowly things began to turn around.[1]

Today Kallestad's church is one of the largest, fastest-growing, and most phenomenal churches in America! The church has come a long, long way from its discouraging beginning. But note, it didn't happen without pain or opposition along the way. It didn't happen without paying a price and bearing a cross.

Another powerful illustration is in the accomplishments of Robert H. Schuller. There's scarcely room here to list his ministry's achievements. But what of his early days?

Robert Schuller went through a period of bitter struggle. An assistant pastor worked against him, and conflict resulted within the congregation. Unrest and criticism bubbled to the surface. He remembers "secret meetings were held, accusations made." About this time, it became evident the church needed to relocate, and this became an issue for the opposition to rally around.

Michael and Donna Nason report:

> He [Robert Schuller] could see his dream breaking apart before his very eyes and often felt helpless to stop it. His assistant was a called minister. He had no ability to fire him. He could be let go only by action of the consistory, and even that had to be on the gravest of grounds. The fact that he disagreed with his senior pastor on nearly everything was not an acceptable reason, and no one knew that better than Bob.
>
> The power struggle went on for nearly two years, sapping the vitality and enthusiasm out of Bob until there was practically nothing left. One night he was startled out of a restless sleep, adrenaline pumping through his body as if his very life were threatened. "Jesus, I claim to know You. I tell others that You are alive. But I don't really know You. I've never really touched You. What do You want from me? . . . Jesus, if You are really alive, if You can hear me, heal me. Heal me before it's too late. Reach into my brain and take out this terrible compulsion, this insanity. Deliver me from myself, from my obsessions, my anxieties. Please."
>
> And he lay there overcome. In a moment, under the bones of his skull, he felt it. Another dimension, another presence

from beyond time and space. A finger pressing, probing into the gray matter. He could feel the flesh separate to give it room as it delved deeper. Slowly he could feel that icy finger begin to ascend back toward the crown of his head; it was dragging something behind it. It passed behind his bones, lifting the psychic poison through his skull. Gone. The darkness was gone.[2]

Elsewhere, Schuller has portrayed that period in his ministry and the early struggles he faced. "For these two years, I went to my study under the enormous weight of an awareness that nearly half of my people were violently opposed to the direction in which I was leading the church. For a period of a year and a half, I would have relished nothing more than a fatal heart attack. In that way, I would have been removed with honor from the unhappy scene! Nevertheless, we had to move ahead."[3]

The Nasons, in chronicling this difficult period, shed light on the emergence of one of Schuller's most-quoted sayings.

> One night, after he had spent hours in prayer, Bob grabbed a pencil and a piece of paper and wrote down the words that God gave him, his own battle cry as a Christian soldier. They would become his testimony of God's faithfulness. St. Paul wrote, "Out of your weakness shall come strength." Robert Schuller took this concept, paraphrased it in modern English, and called it the Possibility Thinker's Creed.

"When faced with a mountain,
I WILL NOT QUIT.
I will keep on striving until I climb over, find a pass through,
    tunnel underneath, or simply stay and turn the mountain
      into a gold mine,
    with God's help."[4]

The rest is history!

Walt Kallestad and Robert Schuller have their stories. I've known similar times of difficulty, challenge, and stress. I've been there. I know the pain, the confusion, and discouragement. I also know each time I received leading from the Lord. Each time, when I was willing to submit to his will and bear my cross for the cause of Christ, he got me through!

Patience in Trial by Fire

Looking back, I can identify two critical times in my ministry. Either time I could have seen all my congregation's efforts come to naught. The first came toward the end of my second year at the Connecticut church. As usual for the first two years of one's ministry, there was the testing period, the wait-and-see period. This is par for the course. That people would be waiting, sizing up their new minister, is "normal and predictable human behavior," as Lyle Schaller would phrase it. People are people, and they need time.

When I was called to that church, some members felt one of the associate ministers who had been there several years should have been chosen instead. Although he left at the end of the first year, others remained who looked upon me as an unwelcome intruder. I understood but persevered.

Some, sensing a rather different style in my leadership, decided they didn't like it. It came to my attention that some of those people were meeting quietly, or should I say secretly, in homes, to plan—I'm not sure what. While I knew this was going on, I decided to ignore it and let things work out. I didn't want to make an issue of it or to appear unduly touchy.

However, another staff person on board for fifteen years prior to my arrival, rather consistently resisted everything I tried to do, even what I considered the simplest requests. In fact, he made it clear to me, almost from the first, that I shouldn't expect him to do anything more or anything differently than he'd done previously. Subtle and not so subtle resistance persisted, despite countless efforts on my part to reach a reconciliation and get him on the team. Meanwhile, many of those people who resented my arrival were clustering around this one person. His cause became their cause.

I took steps to bring the lay leadership into the situation. A personnel committee was formed; there had been none before. The chairman of that committee, the chairman of the deacons, and the president of the church board conferred at length, informed themselves of the situation, and realized they had to deal with things. They attempted to do so, but with little success since the person in question refused to meet with them.

"Too busy," he communicated by a note.

Then, suddenly and abruptly, this person resigned. At once, we had a crisis. Many people, not knowing what had been happening behind the scenes, were troubled and bewildered. With a resignation pending, the church board had to respond. The president, a gentle and caring soul, but also wise and perceptive, let it be known that anyone who wanted to speak before the board at its meeting would be welcome. Many came, some thirty to forty, to voice their protest.

It was clear that this was a critical showdown. Everything I was trying to do was at stake. It might all go down the drain and I might be out. Before the meeting I with-drew into my study. I spent a half-hour in prayer, asking the Lord to help me through this and to give me the poise and patience to endure it sensitively and undefensively.

Just as I was concluding my prayer time, I reached for my Bible and opened it randomly. I was confronted with Paul's second letter to Timothy. If ever there was a timely and pertinent message for me, there it was! I read 2 Tim-othy 4:1–5 (RSV, italics mine); I felt the Lord giving me his directions, his orders.

> I charge you in the presence of God and of Christ Jesus who is to judge the living and the dead, and by his appearing and his kingdom: preach the word, be urgent in season and out of season, convince, rebuke, and exhort, be *unfailing in patience and in teaching.* For the time is coming when people will not endure sound teaching, but having itching ears they will accu-mulate for themselves teachers to suit their own likings, and will turn away from listening to the truth and wander into myths. *As for you* ["you, Morgan," I seemed to hear him say], *always be steady, endure suffering, do the work of an evangelist, fulfil your ministry.*

Equipped with that clear word, I went to the church board meeting, fully assured of his help but determined I'd listen patiently to my critics no matter what was said. I'd remember that our Lord was silent before his accusers, and let the leadership resolve the situation.

For more than one hour, hostile statements were made, accusations leveled, and I was the chief point of scorn. Peo-ple had their say, the board president thanked them, indi-cated the board would now go into session, and that folks were welcome to stay or leave. The board president called for the first item of business, the tendered resignation of this staff member, which was moved and seconded with no discussion. A vote was taken, unanimously accepting the resignation. In that moment, I knew a new era of our church had begun. We had passed over the mountain on the way to the Promised Land!

Hearing this decision by the church board, in fact stunned by it, those who had come to speak their piece got up one by one and left. What I'm happy to add is that in the course of time, most of those people got beyond this difficult period, accepted the outcome, responded to the new direction the church was taking, and became some of my strongest supporters. God was working out his purpose!

The second critical time of testing for my ministry occurred eight years later. The church had grown tremendously. Lots of changes had occurred. More and more people were attracted to our programs.

Our success, however, was proving too much for some people—they weren't sure how they felt about all the new people. They questioned whether many newcomers, from communities near and far, would stay with us permanently. Our services were crowded. Our worship was dynamic. We were being televised from time to time. All in all, things had become different from the old days when the church was quiet and we didn't have the intrusion of being, well, celebrated.

Voices of unhappiness came to my attention. Some—not all or even most—old timers expressed dissatisfaction. I sensed a growing movement of dissenters, and, frankly, wasn't quite sure how to deal with it.

The crisis came late in the spring when a church meeting ran late into the evening. It was evident that some people were unhappy with the drift of things. As well, I took note of worship attendance and made an alarming discovery. Each year we had seen a sizable gain, percentage-wise—except this year. Something had been different. The percentage of gain was slimmer. We were still gaining, but at a markedly slower rate. I took this to be a sign of discontent in some quarters.

The most dramatic moment came when one of my best people walked out of the service one Sunday morning. I can see him to this day. He had been a solid member for years and a strong encourager of mine through most of the changes. But now, it seemed, things were getting to be too much for him. One thing was the television. This meant bringing in bright lights that were distracting. I can't say I blamed this encourager. The lights distracted me, too, but it seemed to be the price we had to pay for people out there to be part of what was happening in here.

In any case, when the lights—or was it the camera?—got too close, this man simply got up, strode up the center aisle from where he was seated, made his way across the back of the church, and walked out the side, or what is called the steeple door. This was all quite visible to me from the high pulpit where I was preaching. In fact, after he was outside, I could see him cross the street and head for his car.

After all these years of halcyon times and steady growth, I had a problem! I knew I couldn't ignore it any longer. I had to do something to reach out to those people.

I began to invite some of them to sit down with me in my study—couple by couple, all of whom I knew to be unhappy. In each instance, there were just three of us alone in the quiet and seclusion. As we talked, I acknowledged that I knew they were upset and asked if they would mind sharing with me what troubled them. I assured them I'd listen, and I did! I schooled myself to keep quiet for upwards of an hour, not to interrupt, not to defend myself, but just to listen.

Each such sharing time brought out one thing or another. For example, several couples felt services were getting too big. They missed the simpler, quieter times without the distractions. After hearing comments like this, I'd repeat what I heard so they would know I listened. I'd share with them what I saw as the great possibilities and promise of the church, and where I felt we needed to persevere. When I felt our church could accommodate a criticism and make some adjustments, I offered to do so. For example, about the earlier complaint, I suggested maybe we should add a new service, an earlier, simpler one, more in keeping with what was preferred. People responded favorably to that, and a few months later we began a third, early service, which was announced as "a simple service."

Once people got a hearing and some accommodation was made, the resistance movement subsided. Within a few months, it was gone. The spirit throughout the church was noticeably improved. In fact, the man who had walked out of church back in the spring surprised me after a service one Sunday months later. As I was greeting people, he came along in the line, gave me a warm smile, and said with enthusiasm, "Congratulations!"

"For what?" I asked.

"You've got the train back on the track and things are going great!" he said. That man remained a staunch and helpful supporter thereafter.

You'll have your days of testing. If you're truly leading the church to be all it can be, you'll have times when you wonder if you can hold it together. What you take to the test will determine what you take from it. The rule is: Pace the growth! Pace the change!

Embracing Change

Among the great ministries of our time, surely, is Jess Moody's. As adjunct professor of church growth at Southwestern Baptist Seminary, he knows something about change. In his ministry through the years he's been a spectacular agent of change. He knows how to go about it, and how to minimize the risks, reducing the likelihood of abject failure. Out of his rich and highly successful experience, Moody discovered and wrote about "16 Facts about Making Change Happen" that are well worth reflection:

> One of the most important elements of church growth is change—not just accepting it, but embracing it. Here are 16 undeniable truths:
>
> 1. Almost all leaders want to move faster than the rest of the organization.
> 2. Your potential opposition will show up within 8 to 12 months.
> 3. Most people can handle no more than three major changes or four minor changes per year.
> 4. Make no more than two major and three minor changes per year.
> 5. Make certain that the two changes are major, vitally germane to the growth of the organization.
> 6. The major change will take two to four years to integrate into the organization, from top to bottom.
> 7. In presenting change, use common words. Don't make them learn a new vocabulary. (Executives love to use the word "paradigm." Down-the-liners hate it.)
> 8. People will adapt to change, if they understand that what they are getting is better than what they have to give up.
> 9. Leaders should let the organization's people know that change is hard for leadership too.
> 10. Don't announce change before you have sold your core group. Sell the center and the circumference will follow.

11. Show by projection how much better things will be five years from now.
12. Project how bad, or slowed down, things will be if the change is not effected.
13. Change is a good time for staff realignment, unless the realignment will cut down too much on the acceptance of the change.
14. Space your changes at least four months apart.
15. Does the particular change build faith, instill hope, and demonstrate love?
16. Salt is a change agent. Jesus said, "You are the change agents of the world." So change it![5]

May I suggest that you commit these sixteen facts to memory? They come from a master in leadership and one devoted to the kingdom and the king. Few have achieved as much as Jess Moody and few have done it so winsomely. They will save you a lot of grief, and they will help you move ahead effectively.

Now look at what it takes as a leader to carry through well as an agent of change: personal traits, qualities, and attitude. These make a world of difference as you proceed and may well determine success or failure.

First of all, in times of change you need patience. Too many pastors and leaders are in a big hurry. They want growth all at once—and they want it today. They find it hard to pace themselves in a way that will go better with the people they're trying to lead. I know something about this, because, frankly, I verge on impatience. Not openly, mind you, but inwardly. I want to be there now! So I must restrain myself. I must manage myself before I can manage the situation.

Second, you need persistence, that ability to keep your eye on the goal no matter what happens. You need to have that capacity to stay the course despite various detours.

Winston Churchill, speaking before the graduating class at Cambridge, kept his message brief and to the point: "Never give up! Never give up! Never give up!" What is that but persistence?

I learned this poem, "Say Not" by Arthur Hugh Clough, years ago and it's been an often timely reminder. No doubt you know it:

> Say not the struggle naught availeth,
>   The labor and the wounds are vain,
> The enemy faints not, nor faileth,
>   And as things have been they remain.
>
> If hopes were dupes, fears may be liars;
>   It may be, in yon smoke conceal'd,
> Your comrades chase e'en now the fliers,
>   And, but for you, possess the field.
>
> For while the tired waves, vainly breaking,
>   Seem here no painful inch to gain,
> Far back, through creeks and inlets making,
>   Comes silent, flooding in, the main.
>
> And not by eastern windows only,
>   When daylight comes, comes in the light;
> In front, the sun climbs slow, how slowly!
>   But westward, look, the land is bright!

Third, you need wisdom and discernment. As you proceed, give careful thought to what you're doing, what you hope to accomplish, and all the factors involved. Weigh them. Be sure nothing is frivolous, impetuous, or ego-driven. Too much is at stake to make bad or unwise moves. Draw upon the wisdom of others, sagacious people in your church, a fellow minister of experience and achievement, a prayer partner. Sometimes things come apart for a leader or pastor because, frankly, what he did was thoughtless. Seek wise counsel, but sense inwardly the way the Lord is leading.

Fourth, you need love. Love will go a long way in many situations. Show that you really care about your people, even those who appear to be against you or thwarting what you're attempting to accomplish. People will forgive a lot if they feel there's genuine love in your heart. Surely you're to love the sheep committed to you, and care if they're hurt, troubled, or frustrated. If you really love them, they'll generally sense this, and many things will get worked out.

In a former church, I discovered a man had become very angry with me. He was intelligent and able, but I think he felt insecure. Something was bugging him, and it had to do with me. He made something of a scene at the church, and I got wind of it.

I decided to phone him and ask if I might come by his home. He said, "Yes," so I immediately headed out to see him. We sat down in his living room with his wife. I began by acknowledging that I knew he was upset, and that I had something to do with it. I asked if he would tell me what I'd done to upset him.

The man proceeded to explain. I've forgotten what the disturbance was about, but I do recall that as we talked, he seemed to be less and less agitated. As I heard him out, I expressed sorrow about having caused this difficulty. I said I respected him, was glad he was in our church, and that any time he was troubled about anything, he should feel free to tell me. We ended this time together in an amicable way. We prayed together, and then I departed. From that day on, that man was one of my warmest supporters.

What had happened? I believe he felt that he didn't count, that he was unimportant. By my going to his home and spending time with him, he began to feel he mattered after all. He sensed I cared about him and valued him, that I had genuine love for him—and I did. That made all the difference. Love never fails.

Fifth, you need faith. What you're trying to do is for God, for the cause of Christ. He needs us to fulfill his wishes. He needs us helping to make his church a powerful force in the world. Trust him to supply you with the counsel and the strength you need, and to surround you with good people who will join the cause and help make it happen.

Here's where your prayer life is indispensable, where you need to protect those times each day spent with God. You need to draw deeply from the well of faith, and that takes time. I could never begin a day without time alone with God, drawing from his Word, being strengthened by his presence and directed by his counsel. You can't lead a church into greater things that will endure without faith— genuine, personal, intimate faith in Jesus Christ!

At such times, you may receive a clear word from the Lord, just as I did before that critical meeting of my church board when the abrupt and bitter resignation of a staff member was to be acted upon, and just as I have many other times. God will speak if you'll listen. There's great wisdom in the well-known, succinct words of Robert Schuller:

> When the idea is not right,
>   God says, "NO!"
> When the time is not right,
>   God says, "SLOW!"
> When you are not right,
>   God says, "GROW!"
> When everything is right,
>   God says, "GO!"

By so pacing the growth and change, will everything go smoothly? Not necessarily. Will everyone stay on board? Not necessarily. At a certain point in one church I was serving, some people did not like the drift of things and nothing seemed to appease them. They just left. This troubled me, and I guess I expressed my unhappiness to one of my key officers, an able, experienced man who held an executive company position. He reassuringly said to me, "Remember, you can't win them all!"

We know from the teachings of Jesus that there's a natural pruning process that goes on with any healthy tree. No less is this true of the church. Some will leave, go their way. All ministers—and I don't care who they may be or how noted they are—have that experience. It goes with the territory. If you've done your best, so be it. Turn it over to God, but stay the course. Keep on keeping on!

10

Celebrate the Successes

So you've come this far, and much has been accomplished. Great things are happening. More and more people are being reached. More and more people are being fed. More and more people are being saved. You went out deeper, and you're bringing in a wonderful catch. The team is being built, and the dream is being shared. What now?

Why, it's time to celebrate, cheer one another, and exclaim together, "This was the LORD's doing; it is marvelous in our eyes" (Ps. 118:23).

Do you realize how important it is to celebrate, and why this is one of the basic principles for leading a vital, growing church? Do you have any idea of the need to tell one another the good news of what's happening in your midst? It can be so soul-satisfying to cheer on and be cheered, all in the name of the Lord. Celebration is a welcome confirmation that we're in this together; rejoicing together is a basic need. Even more—it's a universal need!

A Race Run before Cheering Crowds

My father lived to be ninety-two years old. He took early retirement, you might say, at age eighty-two. Throughout his life he had been an architect, and a good one. He studied at the Harvard School of Design and, during the last decade of his career, was among the architects who worked on the National Shrine of the Immaculate Conception in Washington. But as a young man he'd been a professional bike racer, racing with the best. In fact, his mentor had been the former world champion, Marshall "Major" Taylor, the first great black athlete, whom he vastly admired. My father's love for the "bike game" remained with him throughout his life.

After my father's death I found among his papers something he'd written that reflected this undying love. It was titled "Farewell," and it went like this:

> And now as in days long past, on the old cycle track, its boards glaring white from the bright lights, ten laps to the mile. Again, let the band play and crowds roar as I make the last steep turn and straighten out into the home stretch and cross the finish line for the last time.

What was my father hearing during his last days? Clearly, he heard the enthusiastic crowds, the applause and encouragement from the grandstands. This was a time of great celebration, triumph, and victory. As he crossed the finish line of life, he was being cheered!

What he wrote brings to mind the passage in Hebrews 12. What a glorious picture we find there! The setting, you'll notice, is an arena, and the event is a race—not a bike race, a foot race. Here, too, is the implication of cheering crowds in the grandstands. The angels in heaven are cheering us on! Reflect on that passage and the message it gives: "Therefore we also, since we are surrounded by so great a cloud of witnesses, let us lay aside every weight . . . and let us run with endurance the race that is set before us, looking unto Jesus, the author and finisher of our faith" (Heb. 12:1–2 KJV).

Different translations capture the scene differently. The Good News Bible says: "As for us, we have this large crowd of witnesses around us. So then let us rid ourselves of everything that gets in the way . . . and let us run with determination the race that lies before us. Let us keep our eyes fixed on Jesus, on whom our faith depends from beginning to end."

Can you see that crowd—waving, shouting, cheering us on? What a thrilling, stirring scene! Could anything be more wonderful? Not too different, is it, from the picture my father had in his final days? It is of a cheering crowd, encouraging our eventual and inevitable victory.

Celebration is so much a part of Scripture. Throughout, is a call to celebrate: celebrate the love and wonder of God, the work and presence of Christ, and—yes—one another. Ours is a happy, joyful, celebrational faith, and we need to keep this in mind as it applies to our work as leaders and pastors. Everyone needs celebration, lots of it. That's true of you, and me, and the people we lead.

To me this cheering and celebrating is an integral part of sharing the dream and building the team. A good coach affirms his players from the sidelines, urging them on and cheering for them all the way. Only then can the team play the game well and be assured of victory.

Catch People Succeeding and They Will

Early in my ministry, the third church I was called to serve had gone through a crisis that could only be described as horrific. Without going into the grim details, let me simply say that the church had become about as demoralized as any church could possibly be. People were leaving in record numbers. Finances were falling off precipitously. Some suggested the church should simply close, that recovery was all but impossible. It had been one of the leading churches in the state in its better days. It had been served by several notable ministers, among them George Buttrick early in his career.

When I was called to that church, I was reluctant. In fact, I didn't want to go at first. A minister friend urged me not to, saying he wouldn't send his worst enemy there, let alone one of his best friends. I blurted out in spite of myself, "But who does the Lord's work?" In that moment, I knew it wasn't me speaking, though it was my voice. It was the Lord speaking through me. I believed I'd better take him seriously, too, so, you guessed it, I accepted the call.

Over the course of the next few years the church recovered and thrived, becoming the leading church in the state. As we began our work, I looked for every good thing, good sign, and good development to lift up and celebrate. These people had been thoroughly demoralized. They hardly knew what to believe. They needed good news. So in my communications to the parish via our newsletter, I spoke generously of the good things happening and what wonderful people I knew them to be.

A minister friend in the town north read these communications and was incredulous. In fact, he scoffed. He'd known this church intimately, and some of the things going on there. To him the picture was bleak, without a glimmer of redeeming grace. *What can Morgan be talking about when he speaks so glowingly of these people and this church?* he wondered. But with time he began to understand and to catch on. "Now I see what you are doing," he admitted to me later. "Now I understand why you write those things."

That church and those people needed a new self-image. They also needed to see what good things they had going for them. There was enough of all the grim stuff. They needed to believe their situation could be salvaged and that God was at work in their midst after all. I praised them to the sky, and celebrated every glimmer of gain and sign of the new era bursting all around them. I truly believed that in the grandstands of heaven the saints were cheering, shouting, and waving, wishing us well and urging us forward.

Leaders shouldn't fail to understand this basic need. They shouldn't get so caught up in their critical faculties or so focused on the details that they can't say, warmly and enthusiastically, "Bully for you! You're going great! You're on the way! It's happening! I see God at work in you and in the others! God will have his way here, and he will have his way through you and all the others on this wonderful team!" Such warm affirmation is basic to leading a church into significance and greatness.

This is true not only for a church that's gone through a most disheartening time. It's true of all churches aspiring to be all they can be for the kingdom and for the King. The world is replete with negativity. There are always those ready to find fault, and plenty of disheartening forces at work knocking the stuffing out of people, making them doubt their worth or the efficacy of the church. Surely they need a setting where the atmosphere is uplifting, joyful, and celebrational! If so, look out for every good sign, and be ever ready to celebrate one another and any successes.

Paul set a wonderful example of this. Read his letters. No wonder he played such a role in leading the churches in their incredible expansion. Sometimes he had to admonish the churches and the people to whom he wrote. But a strong and frequent theme is one of rejoicing, commending them for their good works, lauding them for their faithfulness.

To the Colossians Paul wrote: "We give thanks to the God and Father of our Lord Jesus Christ, praying always for you, since we heard of your faith in Christ Jesus and of your love for all the saints; because of the hope which is laid up for you in heaven" (Col. 1:3–5).

To the Philippians he wrote: "I thank my God upon every remembrance of you, always in every prayer of mine making request for you all with joy, for your fellowship in the gospel from the first day until now, being confident of this very thing, that He who has begun a good work in you will complete it until the day of Jesus Christ" (Phil. 1:3–6).

To the Thessalonians, he wrote: "We are bound to thank God always for you, brethren, as it is fitting, because your faith grows exceedingly, and the love of every one of you all abounds toward each other, so that we ourselves boast of you among the churches" (2 Thess. 1:3–4).

Paul was the great encourager and coach to many churches. He didn't hold back rejoicing. He praised people to the skies and cheered for them amid every triumph and victory for the cause of Christ. No one has set a better example of this vitally important aspect of being an effective leader and helping the churches to be all they can be.

In the best-selling book of two decades ago, *The One Minute Manager,* authors Kenneth Blanchard and Spencer Johnson make much of keeping negative feedback to an absolute minimum when dealing with the people one manages. Hold them accountable, of course, the authors urge. Find out what their goals and plans are, and what they intend to accomplish. But if there's anything negative that needs to be said, keep it as brief and to the point as possible. Then get on to all you can affirm and encourage. Practice "the art of catching people doing something right."

In most organizations, the authors point out, "the managers spend most of their time catching people doing what? Doing something wrong. Here we put the accent on the positive," they write. "We catch people doing something right."[1] What immediately follows is the "One Minute Praising." Praise and celebrate what your people are doing.

If this applies to the business world, no less does it apply to churches and the people you're called to lead and to coach. They need the encouragement of praise, to hear others cheering for them, and others celebrating their part in what is happening for good. That's why it's vitally important to celebrate the successes. Don't hold back!

The Good Coach Celebrates

Strangely, I don't remember many on my high school faculty, but I do remember Coach "Doc" Abell. I remember his encouraging us, smiling at us, and always being there to cheer us on! He was the model of a good coach, the kind you wanted to give your best to in return. You wouldn't fail such a man. You had to come through, make that basket, climb that rope, or win that race—for the coach! Why? I learned something from him: what it takes to be on the sidelines, clapping my hands, cheering on the team, and celebrating their every success.

A vital, growing church will have such an atmosphere of enthusiasm, mutual encouragement, and delight in unfolding success. This is an atmosphere to be cultivated and nurtured, for it's the atmosphere that will bring out everyone's best. This is the atmosphere that radiates the joy and faith you have in Christ, and in which the Lord's command to love one another is fulfilled in being together for his cause.

This celebrative atmosphere will profoundly affect everyone concerned. Lay leaders will give of themselves wholeheartedly, devoting time and energy toward what's worthwhile and accomplishing great things for God. Staff people will find fulfillment and feel this is the one place they desire to be even though they may not be the best paid in similar positions. (They should be adequately compensated since the workman is worthy of his hire, but even with tight budgets, staff can feel they are part of something significant. They know God is being served in an exciting way.) Such an atmosphere will call forth the best, and you'll have a wonderful, glorious time along the way.

Ways to Celebrate

There are countless ways to celebrate success. As you welcome people at services, you can speak, without overdoing it, to convey the enthusiasm and joy you find in church. Let it be known that God is among us, his Spirit is alive, and the congregation is composed of people who care about and love one another.

In the printed material of the church, such as bulletins for services, expressions can repeatedly disclose the spirit of the church, suggesting good things are happening and why we rejoice in being a part of it.

In staff meetings, there can be a prevailing spirit of support for one another, appreciation for one another, and delight in one another's achievements and successes. "See how they love one another," it was said of the early Christians. So, too, you can love and cheer and celebrate one another. Believe me, it will make for a far healthier and more enjoyable setting in which to labor for the Lord.

When in any larger gatherings, refer to others on the staff, and let people sense how much you value them, what good things they're doing, how wonderfully the Lord is using them. People will sense that your church is a healthy organization, and it's healthy in the Lord. How much better is that than when representatives of this or that organization make uncomplimentary remarks or engage in put-downs? I've seen that going on through the years in many church organizations, almost *ad nauseum*. Maybe someone thinks it's clever, but it's far from that. It has no place in a vital, growing church that's going great guns for the kingdom and manifesting the Spirit of Christ.

When there are fellowship meetings or department meetings you can lift up the church and speak with transparent enthusiasm of what you see happening. The contagion will spread, and people will find greater joy and fulfillment in being a part of such a church.

When new member meetings are held, it's important that these folks understand the uplifting, rejoicing spirit of the church they're joining. They need to catch the enthusiasm and gratitude prevailing throughout. They need to know for certain that yours is a celebrational church and join in that celebration.

Throughout the total life of the church, there can be a glow of celebration and thanksgiving. You can be as those who know the angels of heaven are rejoicing in what you're doing, cheering you on, telling you to "go for it," giving their angelic blessing!

The Celebration Benediction

In the complex of our New England church, there's a glassed-in walkway called "The Connector," linking three buildings and leading directly to the Meetinghouse. A remarkable feature is that since our building backs up to the ancient village cemetery, along the glass walkway are cemetery stones as close as two feet. When Robert Schuller visited us the first time, he saw the stones and stopped in his tracks, exclaiming, "Wonderful! Wonderful!" Then he added, "My Crystal Cathedral will not be a real church until we have a cemetery!" And so the Memorial Garden of Garden Grove, California, was first conceived.

As I walk toward the Meetinghouse for services, my eyes almost always turn to those markers, remembering the people they represent, most of whom, without a doubt, were devoted members of our church decades and centuries before. For years those people sat in our pews, listened to the Word, baptized their children, married young couples, and bid farewell to their departed. In the spirit of Hebrews 12, I fairly hear them shouting for joy, rejoicing in the flourishing of their beloved church and cheering us on! One of them in particular I know must be rejoicing and praising God, for her name, as carried on her stone, is "Bethankful Wells."

Behind all our successes for the kingdom, all our rejoicing, and celebrating, we know where the credit belongs. Because we do, to fail to celebrate would seem ungrateful. Truly we can say and we can sing, "To God be the glory, great things He hath done," and is doing! Truly we can declare, "This was the Lord's doing, and it's marvelous in our eyes." For behind us, before us, and above us—now and always—is the Lord!

This deeper reality is well expressed in a statue I've seen and admired many times. It's located in Copley Square, Boston, on the grounds of the famed Trinity Church, Episcopal, of which the great Phillips Brooks was pastor over a century ago. There in bronze is the standing figure of that wondrous preacher, his left hand resting on the Holy Bible and his right hand lifted up as though gesturing or giving a benediction. What's most notable and significant is who is directly behind the noted preacher: Christ, full figured and beneficent, with his right hand upon Brooks's shoulder.

What accounted for Phillips Brooks's mighty power in preaching the Word was nothing less than Christ. "Keep close to Christ, Philly," his mother told him repeatedly. "Keep close to Christ!" So he did! And never more than when he preached the gospel. Brooks derived his power from the Lord.

So it is with us. Ultimately and assuredly, we derive our power as leaders in his church from him. We owe everything to him. Only as we are in his will and serving his will can we rightly and effectively share the dream and build the team!

The opening chapter of this book concluded with a prayer, one dear to me from that towering figure who died just a century ago—Dwight L. Moody. I should like to close this chapter with another prayer, this by a present-day inspiring and inspired leader of churches whom I also greatly admire, Stephen A. Macchia, president of Vision New England. This is a prayer he suggests we use to begin each day as a pastor or leader:

> Lord, teach me how to love, and serve, and lead as you have modeled and taught me. Help me to focus on the needs of those on the team who are working diligently at the tasks at hand. May my agenda be subservient to the agenda of others. May my words, attitudes, and actions convey my sincere love and appreciation for those who tirelessly serve by my side. Give me the strength and wisdom to lead as you would lead through me. Express your unfailing love through a vessel that often fails others, not because I always choose to but because of my sinfulness that keeps the focus on me rather than on them. May my ministry to the team today be likened to a towel, some water, a basin, and a heart of loving servanthood, willingly and cheerfully giving myself away so that they may know and love and serve you more dearly. For Jesus' sake and in his name I pray. Amen.[2]

Conclusion

Go for the Wow Factor

I genuinely believe that faithfully following these principles will result in a church that will bring glory to God and dramatically enhance the effectiveness of the mission of Christ committed to us. So through it all, go for the best. Seek the highest and the finest in all that you do and in every aspect of your church. Keep quality control in place at all times. Don't settle for second best or shoddy work where the church of Christ is concerned. Stand back and ask if what you're doing is worthy of the Lord we all serve. The church can ill afford what fails to bring luster to the cause you represent and the God you honor. The world will quickly detect what you're doing and presenting as second-rate, if it is.

In the business world, quality control is strategic. I thought of this when my family bought a new refrigerator. The new appliance was delivered, installed, and the old one taken away. The delivery men left a sheet of paper that asked how we rated the delivery service on a scale of one to ten. If it was less than ten, we were to call a certain number and register our dissatisfaction. Twice since the delivery we've received a call from the appliance store asking again for our rating of the service, not only of the delivery but of the entire transaction, from start to finish. People were checking and double-checking, exemplifying quality control!

What about your church? Do you attach such significance in all you do to advance the gospel? Are you as insistent on high quality in your service to the Lord? Are you as determined to make sure your sheep are well and expeditiously served? Is excellence your goal and standard in everything you do and in how your church in all aspects is viewed? If not, why not? Pray, "I will not give unto the Lord less than my very best."

There's another way of putting this: Let's work for the "Wow Factor." In all that you do, seek to shape and fashion your church in such a way that the world can only respond, "Wow!"

Some years ago, a tourist from Texas was driving through the outskirts of St. Petersburg, Florida. Suddenly he slammed on his brakes, looked with astonishment, and then exclaimed, almost prayerfully, "Look at that!"[1] He was looking at the Pasadena Community Church of which J. Wallace Hamilton was then pastor.

The spacious church structure of Spanish design was surrounded by acres and acres of parking space, which was filled at the time. Many people were sitting in their cars, even while the church building itself was filled, listening to and participating in worship via speakers attached to their car windows. What the Texan was witnessing was a first so-called drive-in church, an extraordinary sight at the time, even to a Texan. There, truly, was an exciting church!

Surely you want all who observe you to be impressed with the creativity, excellence, and the painstakingly high standards you've set. You want the only reaction to be that something extraordinary, wonderful, and out of this world is happening.

But should a church be exciting? Let me put it this way: Is there anything wrong with a church being exciting, catching people's attention, making them say "Wow!"? You want this, not for yourself, but for the Lord we all seek to serve—not to call attention to yourself, but to advance the mission. There's no virtue in dullness. In fact, dullness is of the devil. Excitement and enthusiasm are of God! Note that the word enthusiasm (Greek *entheos,* i.e., "God within") means to be filled with the Spirit of God.

Why do 50 percent of Americans ignore the church? Because the church is easily ignored. There's nothing about many churches to suggest that there's anything exciting, outstanding, sensational, or anything that would make someone say, "Wow!" In short, the "Wow Factor" is low!

As you proceed to build something worthy for the kingdom, go for the best where the church of Christ is concerned. Share the dream and build the team in everything you do. Seek excellence. Do that which is "marvelous in His sight" and impressive to behold. Care deeply. Bring honor to our Lord. Reach people so that driving by, they slam on their brakes and say, "WOW!"

To God be the glory!

Notes

Chapter 1: Where There's a Will

1. Rick Warren, *The Purpose Driven Church* (Grand Rapids: Zondervan, 1995), 64.

Chapter 3: Project a Vision Others Can Catch

1. George G. Hunter III, *How to Reach Secular People* (Nashville: Abingdon Press, 1992), 35.
2. George Barna, *The Power of Vision* (Ventura, Calif.: Regal, 1992), 16.

Chapter 5: See from the Outside In

1. Robert H. Schuller, *Your Church Has a Fantastic Future!* (Ventura, Calif.: Regal, 1986), 247.
2. *First Things*, January 2001, 66.

Chapter 6: Lead with an Enabling Style

1. Leadership Network EXPLORER Lite #16, Leadership Network, Dallas, TX.

Chapter 7: Feed the Sheep, Feed the Lambs

1. Warren, *The Purpose-Driven Church*, 299.
2. Hunter III, *How to Reach Secular People*, 59.
3. Quoted with permission of author.

Chapter 9: Pace the Growth—and Change

1. Schuller, *Your Church Has a Fantastic Future!*, 198–99.
2. Michael Nason and Donna Nason, *The Inside Story: Robert Schuller* (Waco, Tex.: Word, 1983), 67–70.
3 Schuller, *Your Church Has a Fantastic Future!*, 34.
4. Nason and Nason, *The Inside Story*, 71.

5. Jess Moody, *CUGM Journal of Church Growth,* vol. 1, no. 1, p. 1, published by Charles Uniting in Global Mission, Apple Valley, CA.

Chapter 10: Celebrate the Successes

1. Kenneth Blanchard and Spencer Johnson, *The One Minute Manager* (New York: Berkley Books, 1983), 42.
2. Stephen A. Macchia, *Becoming a Healthy Church* (Grand Rapids: Baker, 1999), 117.

Conclusion: Go for the Wow Factor

1. J. Wallace Hamilton, *Ride the Wild Horses* (Old Tappan, N.J.: Revell, 1952), 7.

Don Morgan served the First Church of Christ in Wethersfield, Connecticut, as senior pastor for eighteen years. He also worked with churches in Vermont, Ohio, and other parts of Connecticut after serving in World War 2 as a member of the B-17 "Flying Fortress" bomber crew stationed in England and on missions over Germany. He earned his bachelor's degree in psychology (magna cum laude) from Tufts University, and master of divinity from Union Theological Seminary in New York.

He continues to speak and preach across the country; serves as an active chairman emeritus of Churches Uniting in Global Mission alongside its current chairman, Walt Kallestad. He's also a consultant and pastoral mentor to several pastors through the mentoring program of Vision New England.

The author of *How to Get it Together When Your World is Coming Apart,* Morgan has also contributed to three other books, including *Good News from Growing Churches* and *Sermons in American History;* and his sermon, "America Needs Us Now," is part of the bicentennial Congressional Record.

Today he and his wife, Grace, live in a 200-year-old farmhouse on the side of a mountain, neighboring the National Forest in central Vermont. The view, he muses, is gorgeous at this elevation, which is as high as Mount Tabor in Galilee, the possible site of the Transfiguration, and from which the most distant mountain looks like Mount Zion in Jerusalem: "It's as though we are on the Mount of Transfiguration, looking toward Zion."

The Morgans enjoy their six children (three daughters and three sons), sixteen—at last count—grandchildren, and the patient and persistent adoration of a black Standard Poodle named Frieda, who succeeds an earlier and now deceased chocolate brown Standard Poodle named Reinie after the noted theologian, Reinhold Niebuhr, under whom the Rev. Morgan studied when a seminary student.